Teaching the Elements of
Powerful Writing
Using Great Fiction and Nonfiction Models

By Jane Sullivan and Midge Madden

New York • Toronto • London • Auckland • Sydney
Mexico City • New Delhi • Hong Kong • Buenos Aires

Teaching
Resources

Dedications

To my mother, who always believed in me. — *J.S.*

To my dad, the forever adventurer, who taught me curiosity and passion for new ideas and places unknown. — *M.M.*

Acknowledgments

As we began this project, we wondered if we could really accomplish what we set out to do. We decided that it would be worth the energy. And now, months later, the finished product has proven us right. But in the doing, we have drawn from others to keep alive that energy. To name them all would require another book. So we write our thanks here to all those who have supported us: teachers, students, mentors, friends, and loved ones. At the risk of leaving some deserving persons out, we nevertheless would like to acknowledge a few very special people whose encouragement and expertise provided us invaluable assistance. Our editor, Ray Coutu, was as amazing in his support as he was relentless in his critiques. To the master teachers who opened their classrooms to us—David Jackson, Hilari Luck, Kathy Carhart, Diane Groft, and, of course, Sherri Brecker and Karen Flagg—thank you for inviting us in with such welcome. Thanks to the students whose names are scattered throughout the pages of these lessons, and to their parents who generously allowed us to use their children's work. Finally, we owe much to two mentors and role models, writers themselves, who served as our inspiration: Susan Lytle and Susan Mandel Glazer.

Cover design by Jim Sarfati
Interior design by LDL Designs
Cover photo © ThinkStock/SuperStock
Interior photos by Jane Sullivan and Midge Madden

ISBN 0-439-51781-8
Copyright ©2004 by Jane Sullivan and Midge Madden
All rights reserved. Published by Scholastic Inc.
Printed in the U.S.A.
1 2 3 4 5 6 7 8 9 10   23   09 08 07 06 05 04

Contents

Introduction

What I learned about being a writer is you have to work hard and put in your
best effort. From my self-experience, I found that whenever you write, you must
make the reader feel or picture your ideas . . . no matter what."
— Alex Aguayo, 10

Four of us, friends and teachers, sit around the worn, scratched reading table in Karen Flagg's fifth grade classroom in Harlem, New York City. Suspended above our heads, students' finished feature articles hang from a makeshift clothesline. Other students' drafts in various stages of revision lie spread across the table.

"These are *good*, Karen," muses Jane. "Your kids have captured exactly the essence of a feature article. How did you get them there?"

Karen shrugs and then laughs. "We write daily—in genres. We use examples as models. We rewrite—make it better. It took six weeks to finish these articles . . . and, as you can see, some kids are still working on their pieces."

As teachers, we wonder, Can we grow writers? We think back to that day in Karen's New York City classroom. Her students, children of Harlem, had written strong pieces, well documented and well argued. But in Karen's words, it had been a "long, arduous journey." She had led the way, showing students how to write in a specific genre. And they had achieved success.

But *how* had she succeeded in moving her fifth graders from reluctant writers of formulaic products to writers of convincing, well-crafted, and *interesting* pieces? Returning again to Karen's classroom and replaying our discussion from that day, we rethink now this question, a question that became our central idea for this book: What is it that teachers must do to help children *want* to write and to become *good* at writing?

Again and again we listen to teachers' concerns about teaching writing. "What new writing prompts can you suggest?" "What kinds of mini-lessons will help my students pass writing assessments on state tests?" "How can I teach writing when I don't have time in the day?" We watch teachers grab tightly onto new writing prompts, follow a prepackaged program, and still students' writing does not improve.

Teaching elementary students in the 1970s, we had grappled with similar concerns. We had worried that we were simply teaching the mechanics of writing. Our students dutifully churned out teacher-topic, grammar-perfect pieces of writing, but we knew something big, something critical, was missing. Looking back, we had had no inkling that children could learn to write moving, even sophisticated, complex pieces. They were children, after all. Children aren't ready to write beautiful prose or poignant poetry . . . or so we had thought.

How mistaken we were! Discovering the work of Donald Graves, Lucy Calkins, Georgia Heard, and Nancie Atwell in the 1990s, we began to study children's writing more closely. We began to listen, really listen, to children's voices. And we learned that given time and choice of topic, children *write*. Excited, we pushed our thinking further and asked, "How can we help children to write *better*?"

We began to rethink what we understood about the teaching of writing. We each had just developed a writing workshop, Jane for teachers and Midge for college freshmen. The more we wrote and taught writers, the more passionate we became about finding better ways to teach writing. Together, we pored over the research of teachers from Lucy Calkins's writing project in New York City, and were particularly

impressed with the work of Katie Wood Ray and Isoke Nia. Their beliefs that writing could be taught using examples from literature and that students could learn complex crafting techniques fired our imaginations. Touchstone texts. Mentor texts. Teaching writing through genre studies. Brilliant! We thanked Lucy, Katie, Isoke and all the wonderful teachers who had "tried out" genre studies in their classrooms. And then we began.

We worked in tandem, two teach-

ers pushing to understand more about the intricacies of teaching writing. We taught individual students, and observed teachers and students engaged in memoir, fiction, and nonfiction writing projects. We paired with two dynamic classroom teachers—Karen Flagg and Sherri Brecker—who showed us how well children could write if *taught* well. A part of this book is Karen's story of young writers at P.S. 242 in Harlem. Another equally important part is Sherri's story in a small rural school in Westhampton, New Jersey. Very different students from very different backgrounds with one common element—they can all *write*. This book is our attempt to understand what we have learned, and to share with you the possibilities and the power of teaching writing through the genres.

DEFINING GENRE

For the next few pages, we invite you to take a mind-walk with us through our text. We hope to provide the layout and framework as well as to anticipate (and answer) questions that you may have.

We begin with unpacking the word *genre*. When we talk about genre, what do we mean? What do authors intend when they choose to write in a particular genre?

Webster's New Collegiate Dictionary defines *genre* this way: "a distinctive type or category of literary composition." Distinctive. Serving to distinguish. That made sense, but we sought further explanation. We turned to literacy expert Bernice Cullinan, who organizes her book *Literature and the Child* (1998) along genre lines. She explains her decision to use a genre framework in this way: "Literacy forms provide a frame of reference for the student of children's literature; they help with the task of presenting literature in meaningful and varied ways. . . . Genre groups share common features, such as type of characters, settings, actions and overall form or structure [and] distinguishing features help categorize the genres" (p.6). We put our heads together. "What is the advantage of teaching writing through genre?" we asked. We decided that writing in a genre is a little like following a blueprint. The final result is your own but you've based it on a well-tested plan. If, for example, we want our young writers to express an opinion, we show them a plan

that supports opinion: a literary essay or an editorial. Conversely, if those writers seek to entertain, we guide them through the genre of memoir or fiction. We believe that if the purpose of the writing defines the genre, then when we teach within a specific genre, we are not only teaching writing, we are also teaching a framework that will fit the writer's purpose.

We include only three genres in this book: memoir, fiction, and nonfiction. These are the genres that we use as models in our writing classes from second through fifth grades. These are the genres, too, most commonly found on mandated state assessments.

A final comment. It is not our purpose in this book to describe an entire genre study. Isoke Nia, for one, has done that brilliantly in her professional writing and in workshops that she has given across the country. Rather, we wish to provide examples of whole-class lessons that we use as we take our students through such a study.

PLACING CRAFTING DEVICES WITHIN SPECIFIC GENRES

In his book *On Writing Well*, William Zinsser points out that good writing "has an aliveness that keeps the reader reading. . . . It's a question of using the English language in a way that will achieve the greatest clarity and strength" (p.6). We agree. Aliveness, clarity, and strength are characteristics we look for in all writing, regardless of genre.

To help students cultivate these characteristics in their writing, we have selected certain crafting lessons to teach within each genre. We have placed these lessons where we think they make the most sense. For example, in the fiction genre, there are many examples of descriptive details; thus, in the fiction chapter, we provide a lesson on ways to include specific details based on the five senses. We accept that sensory details enhance not only fiction but other genre writing as well. But we also believe that teachers must first show students how to craft them in the genre in which they most frequently appear before using them in other genres.

WAYS YOU MIGHT USE THIS BOOK

We invite you to use this text as an inquiry into the art of writing well and teaching writing well. The book documents our journey as we sought to better understand what writers do and what teachers can do to "grow" students into writers. Our purpose is not to prescribe a writing curriculum. It is to show the possibilities open to teachers in classrooms where students write. We have learned that our students' writing must drive our curriculum. We must first ask, "What is it that my students can do now in writing?" Then, we push further: "What can I teach them to make their writing better?" And then we teach!

We beckon you into different classrooms, and we encourage you to read with a critical eye, juxtaposing your unique classrooms with those described in our chapters. "What might work with my students?" "How

might a lesson be adapted to my own young writers?" These are questions we hope you might ask as you work your way through the book. Using our lessons as models, create your own. In these lessons, we follow, and suggest that you do as well, an order recommended by Australian literacy expert Don Holdaway and others:

- *demonstrate* the task;
- invite students to *participate* with you in carrying out the task;
- allow them time to "try it" or *practice*;
- *perform* the task independently.

This is the common-sense order that effective teachers follow.

THE STRUCTURE OF EACH CHAPTER

Portrait of a Classroom Where the Genre Matters

We begin each chapter with a portrait of a teacher and students engaged in a writing task or crafting lesson. We piece together these portraits in much the same way one would piece together a patchwork quilt. Written observations of classroom contexts, notes documenting the teacher's and children's actions, transcripts of the children's comments and teacher's words are all assembled and carefully woven together into an artistic whole. The idea is to paint a writing scene, to capture a writing moment. The idea is, too, to capture *you*, our reader, enticing you to turn the page and read on.

Characteristics of the Genre

We follow the portrait with a description of the genre—what characteristics might one expect to find in an essay, for example, but not necessarily in a personal narrative? What distinguishes one genre from another? As readers, we should be able to say to a writer, "Oh, I see you are writing a poem," or "This is a good beginning for your expository piece." We teach certain distinctive characteristics of each genre so that students can find them in their own writing and in the writing of others. We also teach students that overlap among the genres does exist.

Examples of the Genre in Children's Literature

Successful authors say that they learned to write well by studying authors they admire. Here we list mentor texts that we have introduced to students as models of the kind of writing they are attempting. A longer list of such books is included in the appendix.

Techniques Writers Often Use in the Genre

As we explained earlier, we place crafting techniques within certain genres, not because they belong there exclusively, but because we feel that it is the logical place to address that particular technique. Thus, in the section on memoir, we address storytelling as a moment in time; in writing fiction, we practice stretching a moment; and in creating opinion pieces, we stress the use of examples that support one's view.

Lessons in the Genre

In the final section of each chapter, we provide sample lessons that we, or one of the teachers we have mentored, have used in the classroom. Each lesson description reads across two columns. The first column lists the steps we followed in executing the lesson and the rationale that explains the purpose or comments on each of the steps. The second and wider column contains narrative that takes you from the beginning of the lesson to its conclusion. You will also find "idea boxes" with helpful hints that encourage revising or editing, and suggestions for how to use the lesson with younger students.

Our intent in this section is to provide you with examples of effective teaching. Espousing a "cookbook" approach, we share ideas about teaching within a certain genre, demonstrating the step-by-step methods that we used. We urge you to look first at your students' writing, then use, expand, or modify our lessons to create your own. Our students may not have needed a specific lesson on describing a setting, or we may have chosen not to emphasize that particular crafting technique in memoir. You, on the other hand, may want students to write better descriptions. There is no single curriculum that fits all; it is up to you to make informed decisions about the kinds of writing lessons you will teach. Writing is an art, and, like music, dance, and painting, there exists no one formula that, followed precisely, brings us to the final, correct product. In writing, there are no absolutes. And wouldn't it be boring if there were?

Chapter 1:
Writing Memoir

PORTRAIT OF A CLASSROOM WHERE MEMOIR MATTERS

In Kathy Carhart's class at William Winchester Elementary in Westminster, Maryland, fourth graders sprawl in various positions on the worn, multicolor rug, listening intently to *Hattie and the Wild Waves* by Barbara Cooney. At the story's end, Hattie, the main character, announces, "I'm going to be an artist . . ."

"I hope she does," sighs Gia. "And I hope her mom will finally understand."

"I do, too, Gia." I nod as I close the book, stacking it with others on the memoir table.

"Hmmm," I wonder aloud. "We've read and shared lots of memoirs over these past two weeks. Let's see. *When I Was Young in the Mountains, The Pain and the Great One, Owl Moon, Hairs* . . . what else?"

Hands shoot up.

"What about *Wilfrid Gordon McDonald Partridge*?" asks Shauna.

"And *My Rotten Redheaded Older Brother*," laughs Kevin. "That was the best!"

"Don't forget the Roald Dahl story we read, *Boy* or something like that," reminds Ernie.

I laugh. "You guys really have been paying attention! Now think about your own writing. Think about the personal stories that you've been playing with, trying to make better. What do you think we need to know before we can turn all your little stories into one long memoir? How did all these authors do that?" I pull out one of Jean Little's memoirs from the stack, casually flipping through.

"Write more stories?" ventures Melissa.

"Yeah, maybe we just need to keep adding stuff from all parts of our lives," agrees Jake.

Suddenly, Jared loudly announces, "Hey, I get it! I get it! Remember when she [Jean Little] says that a memoir isn't a whole head of hair, but only one or two strands of hair?"

I nod.

"Well, that's it. That's how we have to think about our writing here. All those memories we've been writing about . . . well, we're not really writing every fact about our lives, but just those special moments that stick out . . . you know, the ones that we always think about."

"Yeah," chimes in Alex. "We're just letting others peek in at parts of our lives and we have to put these parts together. But that's the hard part, I think."

I smile. "You're really thinking, now, guys. Just as Alex said, remind yourselves that you're giving the reader little glimpses of your lives. Today, if you're ready, let's work on putting together the strands of hair that we have each chosen. I'll come around and listen to your ideas and your writing."

Moments later the classroom buzzes with activity as the children settle into their work. A visitor enters the room, then hesitates, unable to find either the teacher or me. We have disappeared, swallowed up in the melee of young voices and scribbling authors.

Two boys huddle on the sofa, one reading, the other giggling quietly.

"That's really funny, Jake. And it's true, right?" Jack asks.

Jake solemnly shakes his head. "Yep, my mom told me 'cause I couldn't remember all the details. Does it make sense?"

"It makes me laugh, so I guess it does," Jack muses. "Now let me read you my funny memory."

Across the room, three girls march purposefully to the writer's wall where hearts dangle from pink satin ribbons.

"Look, here's my happy memory," Shauna points. "I remembered it after Dr. M. read us *When I Was Young in the Mountains*. It's my happiest time with my dad when we camped in the Shenandoah. Cynthia Rylant's book and her mountains reminded me of that."

Her friends nod, then find their hearts and share their memories.

Two heads bend over a stack of books. Jon looks up as I walk by. "We're making a list of all the memory stories in every one of these books," he volunteers proudly. "George thinks our memoirs can only have two or three memories, but I think they can have more. I'm trying to prove my hunch."

"Good thinking, Jon," I comment. "But what's your purpose here? How is what you're doing now going to connect to your writing?"

"Aw, c'mon, Dr. M. You know! I need to because I want to include all my six memory stories in my finished piece!"

Alex gently taps my shoulder and whispers, "Could we have a talk? I think I've finished a memory story and I'm ready to read it to you."

"And I'm ready to hear it, Alex! I know you've been working on this for a few days now." We find a quiet spot and settle cross-legged on the rug. Alex pulls a creased paper from his notebook, smudged with many cross-outs.

He murmurs, "This is my fourth try, you know." Then, he begins to read:

> Once on a cold Christmas morning, I remember the first present I opened was a star charm with two crystals and a bow. When my mom gave it to me, she said, "You are my star and always will be." Our Christmas tree was brimming with cat ornaments. When we were opening the ornaments, I noticed how pretty they were. Some had spirally glitter. Some had a bell inside a bell inside a bell inside a bell inside a bell. There were lots of cat ornaments. Some cats were flying fish kites, some had mouse parachutes, some were stuffed and soft, some were wooden and solid, and some were made of glass. One cat ornament was a picture frame with my photograph in it.
>
> Once on a cold Christmas morning, our family was together for the last time. I remember my Nana and my Aunt Naomi being smoking "buds" out on the porch. Aunt Naomi had an Internet boyfriend named Duke whom I've never seen. Aunt Naomi also loved to take me to the river and feed the ducks. Nana had a dog named Sunshine. He would always have little squeaky toys that I would always squeeze and he would wonder what the noise was. I remember some of the toys were things like a squeaky frog and dinosaur. I miss Sunshine.
>
> I miss Aunt Naomi and Nana too. Aunt Naomi with her wigs that I loved (as well as her bears) and Nana with her dog, Sunshine. Now they're both stars in the sky.

I sit quietly for a few moments, moved by the beauty of Alex's language and the image of his beloved Nana and Aunt Naomi as stars in the sky. A heart story. A window into Alex's life that opened a piece of his world to me. I am wowed by the power of his words and gently nudge him to the author's chair to tell again his beautiful heart story.★

In this classroom, students shared their lives through their writing, a sharing that caused a change in the class itself. Beginning simply with short memory stories, these children read, wrote, then read and wrote some more. They listened to one another's words and to the words of

★ See Appendix C for complete text of Alex's memoir.

beloved and newly found authors. They completed beautiful memoirs that transformed a group of ten-year-olds and two teachers into a circle of intimacy, and a concrete-walled space crowded with odd-sized desks into a nurturing place in which to write. In this classroom, writing mattered.

CHARACTERISTICS OF MEMOIR

What exactly is a memoir? It is easier to say what it is *not*: a biography, a list of events, or a drawn-out "last-summer-we-went-to-Disney-World-and . . ." chronology. It is a moment in time, an opening in the window to our hearts that allows others to peek inside, to live through that moment with us. As Isoke Nia has said, "While personal narrative is simply a story, a memoir has to have a 'lens.' It is a combination of an 'I'—the narrator—and the lens—the person, place, thing, idea through which the person is telling this particular vivid memory." (Rowan University Educational Institute Workshop, August, 2002).

In her book *Looking Back*, Lois Lowry shares a moment. She tells of finding, at the tender age of six, what she thought was "a very cold mouse, asleep." She tells of arriving home and laying "him gently in the oven" to warm him, and of her mother's discovering what turned out to be a long-dead rat there. Of her mother's loud scream, Lowry writes, "I have always felt that she overreacted." The *I* in this story is Lowry, the *lens* the "sleeping mouse, aka rat." A moment in time. A window to her heart. A memoir.

EXAMPLES OF MEMOIR IN CHILDREN'S LITERATURE

Authors have been generous with examples of this genre. They know that the best writing comes from personal experience. We look for examples that are short and filled with details. In *Looking Back*, Lois Lowry writes brief memories connected with photographs that make wonderful examples for our students. Cynthia Rylant's *When I Was Young in the Mountains* is another book my colleagues and I have used as a model. Rylant provides a repetitive pattern students can use in their own writing. In "Learning the Hard Way," an excerpt from Eloise Greenfield's *Childtimes*, Greenfield's mother, Lessie, builds tension dramatically until we reach the ending, which she skillfully crafts to take us back to the beginning. Michael Strickland's *Haircuts at Sleepy Sam's* has the sense of memoir. While the seemingly simple tale tells us of the Strickland brothers getting "cool" haircuts, between the lines Michael uses the haircuts as a lens that reveals the warm personal environment in which he grew up. In all these stories it is easy to identify the lens through which we observe something of the author.

TECHNIQUES WRITERS OFTEN USE IN MEMOIR

As teachers of writing, we guide students to find these moments in time. Gina wrote about the two weeks her cousins spent with her at the shore, rather than a moment in time. She needed to identify one

14

significant incident within the many that happened and examine it, as through a lens. With my help, Gina found her lens. "You have so many stories in here, Gina," I said. "Which event would you like to write more about?" Gina chose the swing ride at the amusement park in nearby Ocean City. It was important to her because she was scared to go on that ride, scared she'd act like a baby in front of the older cousin she so admired. We explored the depths of her story together, chatting about details that told of her fears, her courage, her tenacity. "That is your story, Gina," I told her. "Write it so that we can see how you think and feel."

The following lessons illustrate some of the crafting techniques students might use to write better memoirs. We want them to narrow the focus of their piece as Gina did, to concentrate on one important experience. We stress the need to include "actions, dialogue, thoughts, and feelings" in order to "show, not tell." We want students to create pictures with their words. In his book *Show, Don't Tell* (1991), William Noble writes, "The stage is where we do our work, and the story is what we try to develop. Standing to the side and explaining things—lecturing—is not dramatic or exciting or entertaining. It is telling and not showing."

The techniques our lessons describe—beginning-middle-end and staying on topic, for example—apply not only to the study of memoir, but to most genres. In fact, when necessary, we review these techniques as we develop pieces in other genres.

MEMOIR LESSON: Telling a Story That's Important to You

Taught by Jane Sullivan in David Jackson's fifth grade class,
Upper Township Elementary School, Upper Township, New Jersey

When you write about what you know, you write from the heart. We always try to get students to believe in that statement because it is a fact of life. As they become more competent, we encourage them to invent settings they have never visited, characters who are but figures in their imaginations, problems they have never experienced personally. As Stephen King advises in his book *On Writing*: "The heart also knows things, and so does the imagination." For now, however, we want our students to write personal stories, stories that they have lived through. Kathleen Tolen is a staff developer in The Reading and Writing Project at Teachers College, Columbia University. In a workshop, she shared the technique this lesson is based on. We've used the approach to demonstrate the importance of focusing on a moment in our lives and staying with it.

PREPARATION AND MATERIALS NEEDED:

- a small container holding various personal objects, one of which will be the source of your "memory" story
- large chart paper or overhead transparency
- a short piece of narrative writing based on the item you select (see page 18)

STEP ONE

Introduce the concept of a "memory box." Stress the idea that the story you tell will allow students to know something about you—the "I" of memoir.

PURPOSE
I want students to feel comfortable sharing personal stories with their classmates. I share my own experiences as an example.

NARRATIVE
I hold up a small box, opening the lid, and say, "This is my memory box. Inside I have all sorts of items that I can connect with a story in my life." I show students various pieces from the box: an origami-folded paper crane, a stone, a pin with figures dressed in Mayan costume. "Each of these reminds me of a story. When I finish telling this story, you will know a little more about me."

STEP TWO

Model by telling the story connected to one of the objects. Simply identify the item, then tell the story.

PURPOSE

My purpose is twofold: (1) telling a story, not identifying the object, and (2) selecting an experience that I have lived through.

NARRATIVE

The students lean forward on their desks. A story?

I select two pieces of a broken sand dollar. "Do you know what this is? It's a sand dollar. Here's my story." I tell them how I found the fragile skeleton in the sand of Hilton Head, put it in my pocket and then forgot about it. Arriving home, I found the sand dollar in pieces. The lesson from this: Take care of things you want to save.

STEP THREE

Allow students to contribute stories that remind them of yours. Keep student participation to a minimum, gathering just a few examples. Assure students you will have a follow-up activity during which they will all have a chance to say more.

PURPOSE

Too much participation slows down the lesson.

NARRATIVE

The children's excitement grows. Hands wave in the air.

"I remember when I left my bike out in the rain, Dr. S.," says Cody. "The next morning it was all wet and I had to dry it off or it would get rusty."

Others share memories that my sand dollar incident awakens.

STEP FOUR

Explain why you chose this particular story. Connect it to writing memoirs.

PURPOSE

I want students to grasp the importance of writing about personal experiences. I also want to introduce the term *memoir*, reinforcing the concept repeatedly during the unit of study.

NARRATIVE

I point out that it is a story in my life. It is an experience that means a lot to me. "I can write stories like that," I say, "and just as you did, other people will read it and think of something like that in their own lives. We call stories from our own lives *memoirs*." I write the term on the chalkboard.

Place your story on the over-head. Show students that although it is similar to the story you told, it is not exactly the same. It is a crafted piece of writing.

PURPOSE

It is important that young writers make a connection between speech and writing. For older students, the writing will be more carefully constructed than the speech. For younger writers, however, they may write the words exactly as they said them. It is our job as teachers to show them how they can craft that writing, make it better.

THE FOLLOW-UP LESSON

I invite the students to bring in their own memory boxes to class for the next writing period. In small groups, they will tell the story connected with one item in their box. Once each student has had a chance to tell his/her story to the group, they will write their stories.

FOR YOUNGER STUDENTS

To adapt this lesson for first and second graders, form groups of three or four children. Assign each child a day of the week to bring in a memory box, and to share the story they choose with the entire class. This will allow you to monitor each child's story. Children can then write their stories with the help of other members of the group.

NARRATIVE

"Here is how I wrote down the story I just told you," I say. I read the short piece aloud. "You can see, it's almost the same as the one I told you. I did choose my words more carefully and tried to make my writing more interesting. Just the same, I wrote my memoir just the way I remembered it happening. I could do that because it happened to me. You could do that, too. Cody, you could write about leaving your bicycle outside and the work you had to do the next day."

Sand Dollar Story
Jane Sullivan

It was a bright morning in November. My friend and I were in Hilton Head, South Carolina, attending a meeting. We walked along the beach near the water, talking and laughing. Suddenly, my friend spotted something in the sand.

"Look, Jane," she said. "A sand dollar. And it isn't all broken, either."

I stooped down and lifted the sand dollar carefully. I turned it around in my hand. It was perfect. "I can't believe it," I said. "I've never seen a sand dollar before that wasn't all broken." I wrapped the fragile skeleton carefully in a Kleenex and put it into the pocket of my jacket. "What a find!"

We hurried back to the hotel and changed so we could go to a meeting. My jacket hung in the closet. The next day we packed our clothes in a hurry and left for the airport. The jacket was in the suitcase now. I had forgotten about the little treasure in its pocket. When I unpacked my suitcase at home, I remembered the sand dollar and reached into the pocket for it. All I found were the shattered pieces. My sand dollar was no longer whole but it was still a treasure—a treasure to remind me to be more careful.

MEMOIR LESSON: Sequencing a Memoir— The Beginning, the Middle, the End

Taught by Jane Sullivan in Hilary Luck's fourth grade class, The Franklin Charter School. Somerset, New Jersey

Often, beginning writers need to develop a sense of order in a story—that every piece has a beginning, which introduces the topic; a middle, which gives details related to that topic; and an end, which brings the piece to a close. If we do not see such an order in a student's writing sample, we recognize our starting point for teaching.

One technique you might use to develop this sense in students is to imagine the story told through a picture. We first draw three squares on the chalkboard and place in the middle box a picture that suggests a story, then ask the students to study the picture. (A Norman Rockwell print often works well.) We tell them, "This is a snapshot, a moment in time in someone's life." We ask them to tell the story they see in the picture, then invite them to speculate. Focusing on the empty square that precedes the picture, we ask students what took place before this "moment in time." Then, pointing to the square that follows the picture, we ask them to tell how they think the story ended—what happened after the picture. As the story unfolds, we record it on three large pieces of chart paper labeled "Beginning," "Middle," and "End." "Every story has a beginning, a middle, and an end," we explain.

Once students grasp this idea, they are ready to move to the related lesson we describe here—telling their own "moment-in-time" stories. We first show them how we can use pictures to tell a story—then write that same story in words. Later, they will write stories without drawing the pictures first.

The exercise described in this lesson took place over the course of an entire writing workshop—the modeling lesson, the writing, and the sharing.

PREPARATION AND MATERIALS NEEDED:

- copies of the three beginning, middle, and end worksheets for each child
- overhead transparencies of the three worksheets for you to model the drawing and writing
- a chart describing the steps in this process

STEP ONE

Remind students of the Norman Rockwell story to help them make the connection between today's lesson and work they have done previously.

PURPOSE
Telling a story through a picture is a little easier than telling it in words.

NARRATIVE

"Yesterday, we told a story we found in the Norman Rockwell picture," I say. "I have a 'moment-in-time' story just like that. I'm going to write my story here. I point to the chart. "These are the steps I am going to follow," I say. "I want to show you how I write a story."

STEP TWO

Distribute the three beginning, middle, and end worksheets that students will eventually use for their writing.

PURPOSE
I want students to become familiar with the parts of the worksheets they will use to write their own stories: the headings Step One, Step Two, and Step Three that indicate the order they will follow; the squares in which they will draw the pictures; and the lines on which they will write the stories.

NARRATIVE

"I'm going to use these three pages for my story. Robert, will you give everyone a copy of these pages?"

Robert gives each student copies of the three pages.

Step One

Step Two

Step Three

STEP THREE

Model Step One of the strategy: Draw the picture of the beginning of the story. Draw simple pictures that do not take much time.

PURPOSE
Drawing details in the pictures reminds beginning writers to include details in their writing. They match their words to the actions they draw.

NARRATIVE
I begin my moment-in-time story by drawing a picture.

STEP ONE: BEGINNING/MIDDLE/END WORKSHEET

Step One

I was riding my bicycle along the road. The sky was blue. The cars were whizzing by. I was singing. I was really having a good time.

STEP FOUR

As you model each step of the strategy, explain exactly what you are doing.

PURPOSE
Modeling and explaining hold students' attention and reinforce learning.

NARRATIVE
"This is the beginning of my story, so I want to draw details that let you see who the story is about and where it happened," I say.

STEP FIVE

Now, write the beginning of the story by matching words to the picture. Write naturally, making changes to improve the writing when necessary.

PURPOSE
I want students to see that I can make "pictures with words."

NARRATIVE
I say the words aloud as I write. "Now you know where my story took place. What words did I use to tell you that?" I say.

Amir picks out words like *blue sky* and *cars whizzing by*.

"Right. You are going to learn something about me from my bicycle ride story," I say.

STEP SIX

Model Step Two. Draw the picture, then write the middle of the story, including details such as actions, dialogue, thoughts, and feelings.

PURPOSE

I want students to understand that writing about what characters do, say, think, and feel is the way we "show" what is happening. In my writing examples, I always try to include these characteristics. In a later lesson, I will show students how to do this.

NARRATIVE

"Now," I say, "let me show you what happened." On the Step Two sheet, I draw the bicycle on the ground and a dog pulling at my leg. "What happened to me?" I ask.

Abena is first to put up her hand. "You fell, Dr. S.," she says. "A dog made you fall."

Let's see if I can write that," I say, picking up the pen. I reread the sentence I wrote. "No," I say, "I think this sounds better." I change it, then continue writing.

"This," I explain, "is the middle of my story. How do you think it will end?"

There are various predictions, ranging from chasing the dog away to going to the hospital.

"Well, let's see," I say, once again drawing.

STEP TWO: BEGINNING/MIDDLE/END WORKSHEET

Step Two

Suddenly
A dog came and bit me on the leg. ran up to me. He barked and jumped around.
    "Go away," I shouted.
    But he wouldn't go away. Instead, he jumped up and grabbed my leg. Then he bit hard. Boy, did it hurt.
    "Ouch, ooch!" I yelled. "Help!"
    I dropped my bicycle on the ground.

Model Step Three—draw the picture depicting the end of the story, then write the ending. Draw out from students what they learned about the author.

PURPOSE

Students need to know that a memoir piece should tell something important about the author.

NARRATIVE

I draw the next picture on the Step Three sheet. The dog, the bicycle, and I are still in the picture. But another character is introduced—a man coming out of the house. I cross words out and insert others.

Satisfied, I say, "Here is the end of my story. What did you learn about me?"

Brandon puts his hand up. "You like to ride a bicycle?" he offers.

"Okay, and . . ." I say.

Isaiah is next to respond. "You're afraid of dogs."

"Maybe," I agree. "Especially when I'm . . .?"

Isaiah finishes, "on a bike."

"Yes," I say, "and I used my bicycle story to tell you that. That's what a memoir does."

STEP THREE: BEGINNING/ MIDDLE/END WORKSHEET

Step Three

A man came running out, and helped me put on a bandage.

"Dutch," he called. "Go away. Get down."

The dog ran into the garage. Then the man helped me up, and washed off the place where the dog bit me. We stopped the bleeding and put a band-aid over it.

Ask students to review the strategy step by step. Record the steps on a chart to which they can later refer.

PURPOSE

Listing the steps I followed reinforces the strategy. Displaying a chart with these steps allows students to use them as a reference guide.

NARRATIVE

I point to the chart that lists the steps I followed. "Let's review the steps I followed. What did I do first?"

As the students respond, I point to that step on the chart. I continue doing this until students have reviewed all three steps.

CHART FOR WRITING BEGINNING/MIDDLE/END STORY

Step One

Draw a picture of the beginning of the story. Write the beginning of the story. Tell *Who* and *Where*

Step Two

Draw a picture of the middle of the story. Write the middle of the story. Tell *What* happened.

Step Three

Draw a picture of the end of the story. Write the end of the story.

SHARING TIME

The lesson is over at this point and the workshop continues with students drafting their own stories while the process is still fresh in their minds. During the "sharing" time, Robert reads his story to the class. Robert is a beginning writer. Yet, in his story, he demonstrates the sense of order that will help him become a better writer.

ROBERT'S EXAMPLE OF BEGINNING/MIDDLE/END

STEP ONE

At my dad's wedding a girl asked me to dance. I thought I could do it.

STEP TWO

When I got out on the dance floor, I was scared to dance. I thought that I was going step on her feet.

STEP THREE

But I followed her footsteps and I didn't step on her feet. I had fun.

FOR YOUNGER CHILDREN

To adapt this lesson for first and second graders, invite one student to share his or her story before asking your students to write individually. As the student tells the story, you or another student can record the picture/story on chart paper. This will allow students to learn by doing while you monitor and prompt as needed.

MEMOIR LESSON: Staying on Topic

Taught by Jane Sullivan in David Jackson's fifth grade class,
Upper Township Elementary School, Upper Township, New Jersey

We usually use webs to show students how to plan a complex piece before writing. In this lesson, the web plays a different role: it is used after writing a draft to discover if the writer stayed with the topic. We show students how the web can be an effective tool for revising.

PREPARATION AND MATERIALS NEEDED:

- blank transparencies
- an example of student writing that is "off topic" (For this lesson, I used Kyle's story "My Fort.")
- chart paper for writing steps in creating a web

STEP ONE

Introduce the objective of the lesson: to practice using a web to check whether we stayed on or strayed from our topic.

PURPOSE

Students can see how an outlining technique such as a web helps pinpoint a problem we may overlook in a simple rereading.

NARRATIVE

"The first time I drove to this school I didn't make that left turn into the school driveway. So, what did I have to do?" I ask.

"You had to turn around and go back," Max answers.

"Have you ever done that in your writing? Lost your way? Forgotten what you wanted to write about?"

Kyle smiles. "I did, in the piece I was writing . . ."

"And . . . ?" I say.

"I knew my piece didn't sound right," he explains. "But I wasn't sure how to fix it."

"Today, I want to show you how Kyle found where he had taken a wrong turn. Where he went *off topic*." I write "going off topic" on a blank transparency.

STEP TWO

Explain that, when we use a web, we write the main idea or topic first.

PURPOSE

Students need to focus on what the piece is all about. Their ideas should then spin off this main topic.

STEP THREE

Draw a web for the first paragraph in the piece. Check to be sure the main idea of the paragraph connects with the topic.

PURPOSE

We need to analyze each paragraph to be sure the main idea matches the overall topic of the piece.

STEP FOUR

Draw one line, or spoke, for each detail. Invite the student to give the details from his writing. Write the details in the boxes at the end of each line.

PURPOSE

The student becomes the modeler, allowing others to see that this is a task within their ability to perform. It isn't just me, saying, "Do this, and this, and this." Using student writing makes a lesson more authentic.

NARRATIVE

I put a copy of Kyle's draft on the overhead. "Here is what Kyle wrote. First, Kyle, what was your topic?" I ask.

"My fort," Kyle answers.

I replace the transparency of Kyle's draft with a blank transparency and write "My Fort" on it as the title.

NARRATIVE

I show the first circle on my overhead transparency with lines branching from it. "Kyle, what did I write here?" I ask, pointing to the center.

Kyle answers quickly. "What my fort looked like," he says. "That's what my first paragraph is about."

"And does that connect with your topic?" I ask, pointing to the title "My Fort."

"Yes," Kyle replies.

NARRATIVE

"And how many lines did I draw?" I ask Kyle, pointing to the spokes on the web.

"Four, because I had four details," he explains. He reads from his draft: *My fort is ten feet tall. It has ladder steps that lead up to the platform. There's a picnic table on the platform and a playhouse at the top.*

As Kyle reads the details, I write them in boxes at the end of the lines.

KYLE'S WRITTEN DRAFT

My Fort

My fort is ten feet tall. It has ladder steps that lead up to the platform. There's a picnic table on the platform and a playhouse at the top.

My friends and I have battles in my fort. We eat, and drink soda and play Pokeman.

My brothers are not welcome in my fort. They are too little and devilish. I try to keep them out but they still come in.

KYLE'S WEB

My Fort

Ladder steps lead to the platform

What my fort looked like

picnic table on the platform

Fourlegs- ten feet tall

play house on top

Playing in my fort

Battles with my friends

played Pokemon

ate and drank soda

STEP FIVE

Check to see if each detail connects with the main idea in the center box.

PURPOSE

Students must learn that, in a paragraph, each detail must "fit."

NARRATIVE

"Okay, now let's see," I say, looking at the class. "Kyle read us details about his fort. Are all these details describing the fort?"

Hands go up. The class agrees that Kyle has stayed on topic.

STEP SIX

Repeat the two previous steps for the second paragraph.

PURPOSE

Repeating the process for the second paragraph reinforces the importance of staying on topic.

NARRATIVE

Kyle explains that he wanted to write some of the things he and his friends did in the fort: *My friends and I have battles in my fort*, he reads. *We eat, and drink soda and play Pokémon.*

Once again we examine the web and check these details. Once again all agree that Kyle stayed on topic.

STEP SEVEN

Continue these steps for each remaining paragraph.

PURPOSE

In the third paragraph, Kyle has gone off topic. I want him to show that he discovered the mistake himself.

NARRATIVE

I ask Kyle to read the next paragraph.

He reads: *My brothers are not welcome in my fort. They are too little and devilish. I try to keep them out but they still come in.*

I write the details on the transparency.

Kyle explains, "I looked at the first two details and I knew I wasn't talking about my fort anymore. I was talking about my little brothers."

"So you took a wrong turn, didn't you?" I say. I show the class the last web on the transparency. Kyle asks me to draw an X through it. It didn't fit!

STEP EIGHT

Provide praise for a job well done.

PURPOSE

Kyle deserved his moment in the sun for solving the problem with the piece himself. An important lesson learned: revising independently.

NARRATIVE

"Yes," I say. "Good job, Kyle. The paragraph was interesting. You might want to use it somewhere else. But it doesn't belong in this piece, does it?"

STEP NINE

Summarize the steps in the process. Write them down on a chart so that students can refer to the steps in the technique when needed.

PURPOSE

"Taking a wrong turn" is not an uncommon flaw in students' writing. It is helpful for them to have a copy of the steps of this technique as a reference.

NARRATIVE

With prompting, students summarize the steps we followed. As they name these steps, I write them down on an overhead. Students make a copy of the chart for the bulletin board.

CHART FOR CREATING A WEB

- Write your topic at the top of the page.
- Draw a circle.
- Write your first paragraph's main idea in the circle.
- Draw lines that branch out.
- Draw boxes at the ends of the branches.
- Write a detail in each box.
- Check: Does each detail tell about the main idea?
- Does the main idea tell about the topic?
- Do this for each paragraph.

FOR YOUNGER CHILDREN

To adapt this lesson for grades 2-3, use a single-paragraph piece. It will make the process simpler.

CHECKING FOR CAPITALS AND END PUNCTUATION IN YOUR WRITING

- Take a green marker/highlighter.
- Put a line under the first word in every sentence of your draft.
- Take a red marker/highlighter.
- Put a line under the last word in every sentence.
- Now check it:
- Does every "green" word start with a capital letter?
- No? Fix it.
- Is there an end punctuation mark (period, question mark, exclamation point) after every "red" word?
- No? Fix it.

MEMOIR LESSON: Writing Dialogue in Memoir

Taught by Jane Sullivan in David Jackson's fifth grade class,
Upper Township Elementary School, Upper Township, New Jersey

Dialogue is an important element of both fiction and memoir. It allows the writer to reveal character traits. It slows down the action. It also allows the writer to show, rather than tell, drawing readers in, holding their attention and making them partners in reconstructing the story. When young writers create stories, they often miss these opportunities, telling about conversations rather than writing the actual words: *He told me he was afraid* versus *"I'm scared," he said.*

We want students to discover the power of dialogue and to learn how to structure it: the indentations, the correct punctuation, and the placement of the attribute markers, or "name tags."

We usually break dialogue writing into several mini-lessons. We first study how a writer constructs dialogue. Then, in a subsequent lesson, we apply that knowledge by writing dialogue. Once students have done this successfully, we show them how to add actions and thoughts to make dialogue more interesting.

The first lesson, learning how writers construct dialogue, is an inquiry. We use text from books students have read. Here, we use a page from my own writing to examine how I set up the dialogue.

PREPARATION AND MATERIALS NEEDED:

- transparency of page of dialogue from a mentor text or your own writing (see sample). The sample text should have examples of the rules you intend to cover in the inquiry.
- black transparency marker
- individual photocopies of the page for students
- large chart paper for creating a list of dialogue rules

DIALOGUE FROM *THE TROUBLE WITH LYING*

The Trouble with Lying

¶ --Paragraph

<u>Quotation</u>

<u>Name tag</u>

¶ By the end of September, Jenny had decided that she didn't like second grade. The work wasn't hard but Miss Bred, her teacher, always looked like she just tasted something bad and she never told Jenny her work was good or smiled when she handed papers back--the way Miss Collins, her first grade teacher, did.

¶ So, one morning on the way to school, Jenny decided to do something about it. The empty lot next to the school building still held bachelor buttons and Queen Anne's Lace. Flowers, Jenny thought. That's what will make Miss Bred smile.

¶ <u>"Cathy, wait,"</u> <u>Jenny called</u> to her sister, who had walked on ahead, <u>"I want to pick Miss Bred a bouquet of flowers."</u>

¶<u>"We'll be late for school,"</u> <u>Cathy answered,</u> frowning at her sister, <u>"Come on! Hurry up!"</u>

¶ <u>"It will only take a few minutes. Look how many I have already."</u>

¶<u>"Two minutes, Jenny. That's all I'll give you!"</u>

¶Jenny set about picking the very best flowers she could find--the ones with all the petals still on, the ones with no brown yet at the tips.

¶ <u>"Jenny. Are you finished?"</u> <u>Cathy called</u> to her.

¶ <u>"Okay, just one more minute."</u>

¶Jenny needed three Queen Anne's to finish the bouquet. She ran to the back of the field to find three perfect ones, then held the bouquet up to the sun. It was a glorious picture of blue and white. She smiled, proud of her great idea, then, looked around and gasped. No voices. No sister. The bell had rung. School had started. And she was late.

j sullivan

STEP ONE

Introduce the structure of a direct quotation: use quotation marks around the words and a name tag to identify the speaker.

PURPOSE
Although readers recognize these structures as dialogue, they rarely stop to examine "how it is done."

NARRATIVE

"Here's a section of a story I wrote," I say. "Let's look at the part where the characters are speaking." I place my copy on the overhead and read it aloud. "The characters Jenny and Cathy are speaking, aren't they? How did I show you what they said?"

"Those commas in the air," Beth says.

"Right, we call them quotation marks," I say. "What's a quotation?"

"Exact words," Marshall answers.

I circle the quotation marks on the transparency and print "QUOTATION" in the margin. Students do the same on their copies.

"What else do you notice?" I ask.

"Jenny's name," points out Cody. "She's talking."

We label that feature "name tag." I record this information on the chart paper.

Parts of Dialogue

- The quotation (What the character said)
- The name tag (Who said it)

Punctuating Dialogue

- Begin and end the quotation with quotation marks ("...").
- If the name tag comes in the middle, use two sets of quotation marks, around the words in the quotation only.
- If the quotation is a question, use a question mark.
- If the quotation shows surprise, use an exclamation point.
- If the quotation simply tells, use a comma.
- Use a period after the name tag.

  Every time the speaker changes, start a new paragraph.

STEP TWO

Examine the punctuation used in quotations.

PURPOSE
Discovering such information for themselves ensures students' learning.

NARRATIVE

"What do you notice about the punctuation writers use in dialogue?" I ask.

We go down the page, underlining the punctuation we find: commas, periods, question marks, exclamation points. Alexa notes that there is never a period between the quotation and the name tag but there are exclamation points or question marks. Others find that a comma often separates the quoted words from the name tag. We add this information to our chart.

STEP THREE

Examine the use of capital letters.

PURPOSE
Students should know that capitals are used in dialogue in much the same way as in other forms of writing.

NARRATIVE

"Let's look at capital letters now," I say. "What's the rule there?"

Students underline the capital letters. Conclusion? They are used conventionally, i.e., at the beginning of each sentence and for proper nouns. Once again, we note this on the chart.

STEP FOUR

Examine the paragraph indentations.

PURPOSE
Young writers often forget to begin a new paragraph when the speaker changes. My goal here is to help them remember.

NARRATIVE

"Let's take a look at the way I indented when I used dialogue," I say. I draw a paragraph marker (¶) at each indent.

Jack notices that every time Jenny or Cathy says something, the words are indented.

We discuss the theory and conclude that, whenever the speaker changes, we begin a new paragraph. We add the information to the chart.

STEP FIVE

Examine where name tags can be placed.

PURPOSE
Typically, beginning writers of dialogue will place name tags the same way repeatedly. They need to learn how to vary their placement. They should also notice that a name tag rarely introduces the sentence.

NARRATIVE

"Look now at the name tags and see what you conclude," I direct.

Underlining the name tags as we go down the page, Max discovers, with prompting from me, that most of the time the name tag follows the quotation.

"Dr. S.," he notes, "sometimes, it comes in the middle." In this example, the name tag never appears first. This goes on the chart.

STEP SIX

Determine when no name tag is more effective.

PURPOSE
Students should discover that repeating "he said"/ "she said" needlessly makes for boring prose.

NARRATIVE

Kelly notices that, sometimes, there is no name tag. We find those examples and I place a check mark before each of the quotation marks that lacks a name tag. I ask how many characters are in that conversation.

"Two," answers Kelly.

"How do we know who is talking, then?"

"They take turns," she answers, "back and forth."

So, we conclude, when only two characters are involved, you do not always have to include a name tag. You can leave it up to the reader to figure it out, or "infer." This is the final addition to our chart.

DIALOGUE CHECKLIST

The rules for writing dialogue can be tricky. A checklist like the one below eases the learning process. Pairing with partners and using their notebooks, students set out to look through the books they are reading for further examples of dialogue. They can find and copy:

- lines of dialogue. Underline the quotation twice and the name tag once.
- examples of dialogue punctuated with commas, question marks, and exclamation points.
- examples of the name tag in the middle.
- examples of an implied name tag.

Later, referring to their individual copies of the chart we created together, students try their hand at writing their own dialogues.

FOR YOUNGER CHILDREN

For students in second and third grade, teach the material over several lessons. Use simpler dialogue and begin with a two-character conversation in "play" format, i.e.:

> *Jenny: Cathy, wait. I want to pick flowers.*
> *Cathy: No. We'll be late.*

In the next lesson, convert the format to conventional dialogue, adding the name tag and the punctuation marks:

> *"Cathy, wait. I want to pick flowers," said Jenny.*
> *"No. We'll be late," said Cathy.*

Once students recognize the parts of a dialogue sentence, the inquiry can continue with other elements of dialogue as needed: indenting, split dialogue, and so on.

MEMOIR LESSON: Writing Strong Leads

Taught by Jane Sullivan in David Jackson's fifth grade class,
Upper Township Elementary School, Upper Township, New Jersey

In *In the Middle*, Nancie Atwell points out that "the lead provides the reader's first glimpse of the main characters and first chance to decide whether he or she wants to be with these characters and read the rest of their story." Students, however, often summarize the entire story in their opening line. For example, as a first-year high school student, I wrote about trying out for cheerleading: *I loved cheerleading and I wanted to try out for the team but I didn't make it.* Too much information, too soon. There is no incentive to read further—we already know how the story ends. By studying how authors write their leads, students learn to craft a lead that will hook the reader. In this lesson, we examine one type of lead: action.

PREPARATION AND MATERIALS NEEDED:
- chart paper with the heading "Kinds of Leads"
- a copy of a good action lead such as Donald Crews's book *Shortcut*
- overhead transparency (or chalkboard) on which is written the lead in *Shortcut*, which has been read aloud from the book the day before the lesson: *We looked. We listened. We decided to take the shortcut home.*
- overhead transparency with an example of a lead you wrote
- blank transparencies

STEP ONE

Reread the lead for the story.

PURPOSE
To learn from mentor texts used as models, students must study the text from the point of view of a writer.

NARRATIVE
"Yesterday we read Donald Crews's book *Shortcut* together," I say. "Now I want us all to look carefully at the way that author began his story." I open the book and read the first three lines: *We looked. We listened. We decided to take the shortcut home.* I put the transparency with those words on the overhead.

STEP TWO

Ask students to analyze the lead to identify the device Crews uses.

PURPOSE

I want students to discover that some leads use action to begin a story.

NARRATIVE

"This is Donald Crews's lead. It's the way he begins his story. What do you notice?" I ask.

There are a few student attempts, which are off the mark—the sentences are short; they all start with *we*. My question was too vague. I rephrase, "Yes, that's all true, but what device does Donald Crews use? What do these three lines tell us about the characters?"

Alexa gives me the answer I am looking for. "What they did?"

"Okay," I respond. "We can call a lead like that *Action*." On chart paper under "Kinds of Leads," I write: "Action—what a character does."

"These are the leads we'll talk about today."

KINDS OF LEADS

Action—Tell what a character does.

Question—Ask a question to start your reader thinking.★

Ending—Give a detail that happens at the end of the story, then tell the story up to that ending.★

Dialogue—Begin the story with something a character says.★

★As we studied other authors' strategies, we added to our chart. Eventually, we added the asterisked leads.

STEP THREE

Ask students to analyze the structure of the lead.

PURPOSE

This lead has an effective structure that students might want to use in their own writing.

NARRATIVE

"Now, let's take a look at the sentences. What do you notice about the way they're written?"

"They all begin with *we*," says Max. "Then the verb comes."

"It has a kind of rhythm," adds Kyle.

Kelly raises her hand. "The first two sentences have only two words. The last sentence is longer."

"Do you think that helps the rhythm?" I ask. I repeat the sentences. The students nod.

"So, we have a short sentence, a short sentence and a long sentence. Leaving a space to add the name of the technique, I print: "writes two short sentences and one long one." Then I ask, "What could we call that structure? Any ideas?"

Beth raises her hand. "Short, short, long?" she asks.

"I like that, Beth," I say.

The others agree. In the blank space, I write "short, short, long."

STEP FOUR

Write examples of other leads with the same structure.

PURPOSE

I want students to see that they can "borrow" the structure of an author's lead and use it to write their own leads.

NARRATIVE

I pick up the pen and face the class. "Remember my memory box and the story about the sand dollar?" I ask. (See page 18.) Students nod. "Suppose I wanted to use *Shortcut* as a mentor text." I put the transparency of my sand dollar story on the overhead and read the lead aloud:

> *It was a bright morning in November. My friend and I were in Hilton Head, South Carolina, attending a meeting. We walked along the beach near the water, talking and laughing. Suddenly, my friend spotted something in the sand.*

"If I wanted to write a lead like Donald Crews's, I'd take out these first two sentences." I draw a line through the first two sentences and read what's left. I draw lines under walked, talked and laughed. "Here are three verbs I might work with. I could write: *We talked. We laughed. We walked along the sand.*" I write that on the transparency.

STEP FIVE

Give students several examples as possible variations on your lead. From these examples, invite students to choose which they think would be the best lead.

PURPOSE

Students should learn to try out several variations of a lead before deciding on one.

NARRATIVE

"What do you think of my new lead?" I ask.

Kelly gives me her honest opinion: "I like the other way better," she says.

"That's a good point, Kelly," I answer. "We need to try out leads, then pick the one we think is best."

"You do get into the action right away," says Jeff. "It takes a while the way you first wrote it."

"Maybe I could try something else," I say. This time I write: "My friend and I were at the beach talking and laughing and walking along the sand when we saw it. A sand dollar. Half buried."

"Can you see what I did there?" I ask.

Cody spots it. "You used long, short, short," he says.

"Yes," I say, "I changed it around a bit to fit my writing, didn't I? We can take ideas from good writers and make them our own. That's what I did here."

STEP SIX

Review the procedure.

PURPOSE
Summing up the steps of a new procedure reinforces learning.

CHART FOR LEADS

- Study Donald Crews's lead.
- Action
- Short, short, long
- Try it out.
- Try it another way.
- Pick the one you like best.

FOR YOUNGER CHILDREN

To adapt this lesson for second and third graders, avoid variations of the model lead. Instead, proceed with a single lead that matches the sample. Give several examples that use the same structure. Invite students to give leads to their own stories, patterned after the model structure.

NARRATIVE

"Okay, so let's recap," I say, putting another transparency on the overhead. "What did we do first?"

"Read a lead an author wrote," was Max's contribution.

"But we did more than just read it, didn't we?"

Max corrects himself. "We studied it. What it meant. How Donald Crews wrote it."

I write: "Study Donald Crews's lead" on the transparency.

"Okay, and what did we discover?"

"That it was an action and that it went short, short, long." Beth says.

I write those two comments. "And then?"

"You tried it out," says Cody.

I add that to the chart I am writing. "And then," I say, prompting.

"You decided to use it?" asks Alexa.

"Hmm, not quite yet," I say.

"No," says Jeff. "First, you tried it another way."

"Good," I acknowledge. "And what do you think I'll finally do?"

"Pick the one you like best?" asks Max.

"Exactly," I say. "I might use the same structure the author used, or I might change it a little."

Students copy into their notebooks the chart describing the procedure. They return to the memoir they are writing and try out this strategy. Later, we share results with the class.

CHECKING SPELLING

If you are writing and want to use a word but aren't sure how to spell it:

Ask yourself: How does the word look? How does it sound?

Write it the way it sounds, the way you think it looks.

Circle it. Come back to it later to check the spelling.

If you want to remember how to spell that word:

Write the word on a strip of paper.

Make sure the spelling is correct.

Say the word slowly, stretching out the sounds.

Look at each letter as you say the word. Do this three times.

Fold the edge of the paper down so that you cannot see the word.

Picture the word in your mind then write it on the paper.

Unfold the paper and check to see if you spelled it right.

If you didn't get it right, study the part you misspelled.

MEMOIR LESSON: Using Your Senses

Taught by Jane Sullivan in David Jackson's fifth grade class,
Upper Township Elementary School, Upper Township, New Jersey

Once students grasp the idea of "showing" their stories through action and dialogue, we introduce the idea of description. While students do use details related to things they see, they often overlook those related to what they hear, smell, touch and taste. This lesson is designed to show students that they can include *all* senses in their descriptions.

In a previous lesson, we studied examples of Jane Yolen's use of the senses in writing. For example, in her book, *Letting Swift River Go,* she wrote such phrases as *the wind whispered softly,* and *the trains . . . , their long whistles lowing into the dark,* and *tasting the thin sweetness of sugar maple sap.* We made a list of these phrases and talked about how the author used hearing and taste. Students drew the conclusion that using such sensory images "completes the pictures in our mind." Now we were ready to create our own descriptions, using the same techniques.

PREPARATION AND MATERIALS NEEDED:

- excerpts from a book with lots of sensory details, written on the chalkboard or a chart (For this lesson, I wrote on the chalkboard the examples from Yolen's book mentioned above.)
- two copies of the "senses" chart listing the five senses on a transparency or large sheet of chart paper (One, the model chart, is filled in; the other, the students' chart, is blank at the beginning of the lesson, containing only the headings. It will be filled in during the lesson.)
- photocopies of the blank chart for each student
- several blank transparencies

Model Chart for the Senses
(completed beforehand by the teacher)

I see	I hear	I smell	I feel	I taste
Oak trees stretching branches to the sky	a crow cawing	---	a breeze beating against my face	---
leaves lying on the ground	leaves crunching	---	aches from stretched muscles	---
clouds floating	an acorn snapping	---		

Student Chart for the Senses
(completed during the lesson)

I see	I hear	I smell	I feel	I taste
My pencil rolling around the floor	Jordan and Vincent whispering	french fries		salty potato chips
a seagull swooping down	seagulls crying	hot dogs	my chair pressing against me	
		wet coats	my pen pressing on my thumb	

STEP ONE

Call students' attention to the descriptions from Jane Yolen's book listed on the teacher chart.

PURPOSE

This step shows students that imagery depends on all the senses.

NARRATIVE

"Let's look at the list we made yesterday," I say, "and review some of the ways Jane Yolen writes description."

We read the examples written on the chalkboard.

"So, why are phrases like these important in writing?" I ask.

"They let you make pictures in your mind," Kelly answers.

"You can see what's happening," says Max.

"I can hear that train," says Beth.

I agree. "A train whistle sometimes sounds like a cow, doesn't it? Today, we're going to put this kind of description into our own writing."

STEP TWO

Distribute the handout of the blank student chart and put a transparency of the filled-in model chart on the overhead, with the details covered up.

PURPOSE

Students will see how they can learn from a writer's use of imagery.

NARRATIVE

"I want to show you how I used Jane Yolen's examples and filled out this chart when I came back from my walk this morning," I say. "First, I listed some of the things I saw along my walk." I move the paper so that students can see the first column. "I wrote 'what it was that I saw and what that thing was doing.'" I read the entries in the first column aloud.

STEP THREE

Have students list several things they see in the classroom or outside on the first column of the student chart.

PURPOSE

Observing a task and then repeating it step by step make learning easier for students.

NARRATIVE

I put a transparency of the blank chart on the overhead and invite students to look around or out the window and tell some things that they see and what those things are doing.

Elizabeth sees "my pencil rolling around on the floor."

"I see a sea gull swooping down," says Maria.

I list these on the transparency. Students copy them onto their charts.

STEP FOUR

Reveal the "I hear" column of the model chart. Be sure students note that the phrase includes the thing from which the sound came.

PURPOSE

In a later step, I will demonstrate how we can take these phrases and turn them into sentences. The task will be easier if the examples include not only the sound but the "thing" that makes that sound.

NARRATIVE

After a few minutes, I continue with the model chart. "Let's look at what I heard this morning," I say, moving the paper to reveal the "I hear" column. "See, here, how I included the noise and what made it," I point out as I read the entries in the second column.

STEP FIVE

Have students give examples of sounds they hear in the classroom. Have them write in the second column of their charts what the sounds are and what produced them.

PURPOSE

As in the previous step, repeating the task students observe makes learning easier for them.

NARRATIVE

"Now, you find sounds we can put on the chart," I say.

Maria returned to her sea gulls to write "sea gulls crying"; Danny hears "Jordan and Vincent whispering."

We add these to the second column of the chart.

STEP SIX

Explain that there may be some columns in the chart that have no entries.

PURPOSE

The object of this exercise is to get students to think about senses other than sight, but not necessarily to fill up the chart.

NARRATIVE

When I move the paper to the side to reveal the third column, students see no entries. "Why do you think this column is empty?" I ask.

Elizabeth raises her hand. "You didn't smell anything?" she asks.

"Right. There were no really outstanding smells along my walk." I have drawn dashes there.

STEP SEVEN

Allow students to make entries in the third column of their charts, if they choose.

PURPOSE
Students should understand that sometimes odors enter the picture.

NARRATIVE

"Now," I say, "you may want to put some items in column three."

"Maybe the cafeteria food?" Jacob suggests.

"What kind of food?" I ask. "Be specific."

"French fries," Vincent adds.

"Hot dogs," says Chris.

Kelly raises her hand. "How about the damp smell from our wet coats. Can we put that down?"

"Sure," I say. "That's a good way to bring your reader into our classroom."

We add those suggestions to the chart.

STEP EIGHT

Fill in the last two columns on the chart. Note that many will not have ideas in this setting for "I taste." My model does not include this.

PURPOSE
Older students will catch on to the procedure after several trials. This allows us to move ahead at a faster pace.

NARRATIVE

"Let's finish up our charts," I say, showing students my entries for "I feel." I ask what two parts I have included in my entries.

Abby grasps the connection: "What you felt and what it was doing," she says.

Acknowledging that, I invite students to give examples of feelings for the class chart.

Jacob offers "The back of my chair pressing against me."

Zach says "I can feel my pen."

"And it is . . . ?" I prompt.

Zach finishes "pressing on my thumb."

We add these. Like the "I smell" column, my "I taste" column is blank. I ask students for examples of taste.

Jordan says "I still taste my potato chip snack."

"And it tastes . . . ?" I prompt.

"Salty," Jordan finishes.

They add that to complete their charts.

STEP NINE

Show students how to turn the items into sentences.

PURPOSE
Students gain a sense of sentence structure, and how to use sensory images within sentences.

NARRATIVE

"Now, let's read what we have in our columns as sentences. Look at the first column on my chart," I say, reading the "I see" heading, then each item underneath it:

I see oak trees, stretching their branches to the sky.

I see leaves lying on the ground.

I see clouds floating in the sky.

STEP TEN

Have students take turns rewriting on the transparency the sentences from their charts.

PURPOSE
This gives students an opportunity to participate actively.

NARRATIVE

"Now, let's do the same thing with your chart," I say. Students take turns writing the sentences on a blank transparency, leaving a space between sentences.

I see my pencil rolling around on the floor.

I see a sea gull swooping down.

STEP ELEVEN

Cross off the *I see* part of each sentence and read the remainder. Note: This step will be easier if a participle (i.e., an *-ing* or *-ed* word) is part of the original sentence.

PURPOSE
I want to show students that the sentence will be stronger without the *I [sense]* lead.

NARRATIVE

"Now, here comes the fun part," I say. "Let's go back to my first-column sentences." I point to these sentences on the overhead. "We're going to cross off the *I see* in the sentences. What do we have left?" Students read the remaining phrases aloud:

Oak trees, stretching their branches to the sky.

Leaves lying on the ground.

Clouds floating in the sky.

"Hmm," I say. "What happened here?"

Jeff raises his hand. "You don't have sentences any more."

"Very observant, Jeff. Can we fix up my phrases, make them into sentences, maybe add more details?"

"You could say: 'Oak trees are stretching their branches to the sky'," says Cody.

Inserting the word *are* into the sentence as Cody suggests, I ask, "Is it a sentence now?"

The students nod in agreement.

"How about the next one? How can we fix that?"

This time Kelly has an answer. "Leaves were lying on the ground, showing off their colors," she says.

By now others begin to catch on and hands wave. "Clouds are making pictures as they float in the sky," is Alexa's idea.

FOLLOW-UP ACTIVITY

As a follow-up activity, students rewrote the other sentences from the chart. Below are the results:

A crow cawing became *A crow cawed to signal to his friend danger was lurking.*

Leaves crunching under my feet became *Leaves crunched under my feet as I walked along the path.*

An acorn snapping when I stepped on it became *An acorn snapped when I stepped on it.*

A breeze beating against my face became *A breeze was beating against my face.*

Muscle ache from stretching became *My muscles ached from stretching.*

FOR YOUNGER CHILDREN

To adapt this lesson for second and third graders, divide the lesson into parts. First, show students how they can fill in the chart. In a subsequent lesson, show them how they can take the "I see, I hear," etc. away and write sentences without those beginnings.

Chapter 2: Writing Fiction

PORTRAIT OF A CLASSROOM WHERE FICTION MATTERS

Sheets of water slide down the tall, fogged windows of Karen Flagg's classroom as strong winds rattle the panes. Bare branches of a lone sycamore swing wildly, reaching eerily toward us as we peer outside. "A perfect day to launch fiction writing," I muse, and motion students to join me on the carpet for writing workshop.

Sitting in the midst of 20 fifth graders, I marvel anew at Karen's ability to motivate these young writers. I think about our many conversations on ways to teach fiction and I silently thank Karen for the invitation to work alongside her in her classroom. I pull out two books, the texts for today's lesson. Students sit with notebooks on laps, pencils poised to begin.

Lights flicker and Joey comments, "Wow, Dr. M.! We could really write about this storm!"

"Hmmm. They have enthusiasm, these kids," I think. "But are they ready to write fiction?" I look across the circle at Karen and smile.

"Yes, we could, Joey," I agree. "Anyone know what we're doing when we focus on, for example, writing about a storm outside?"

"Well, we're kind of telling the reader about a place or something, sort of describing, you know, like when we did . . ." Kelly pauses and looks through her notebook. Laying the notebook on the carpet, she points to the open page. "Here, I've got it! Remember when we wrote poems, those window poems? Well, we had to get a picture of something in our minds and see, hear, and sense things about that mind picture. So we're describing something or someplace to make a picture in the reader's mind."

"Yeah, Kell, you're right!" Jana says. "When Joey started talking about the storm outside, I suddenly got a picture of a scary scene and I remembered Alex's poem 'Blue Eerie Light.' It gives me chills to think about it!" Jana shudders.

"Hmmm. Good thinking, Jana. Alex, can you find your poem? Maybe reread it to us?"

"Sure, Dr. M. Got it right here." Alex begins to read:

> Dull, bright, flash
> of light.
> The sound of
> whispery wind,
> whispery wind,
> whispery wind.
> Where did you come from?
> How did you get here . . .
> What are you?
> My blood boiling,
> my mouth dry,
> my stomach churning.
> I walk up to the light.
> I try to touch it.
> But
> it just fades away.
> What was that eerie
> blue light?

Alex fades his voice, ending in a whisper. The rest of the children are silent.

"So, does Alex's poem paint a picture in your mind?" I ask softly. Heads nod.

"Okay. Now listen to this excerpt from a book by Stephen King. The book is called *The Girl Who*

Loved Tom Gordon. I begin reading, stopping at the line: *When people got lost in the woods they got seriously hurt. Sometimes they died.*

"Keep going, please, Dr. M.!" students beg.

Shaking my head, I close the book. "I'd like you to jot down in your notebooks right now what you noticed about this piece of writing and Alex's poem. Take a few minutes. . . ."

The students begin. Jared scribbles quickly across his page. Dawn stares ahead, then draws two circles in the middle of her page. She writes "Stephen King" in one circle and "Alex" in the other and begins to web her ideas. Kelly chews on her pencil as she jots ideas down in list form. Students work independently in their notebooks, clearly absorbed in their work. I move to the center of the room and switch on the overhead.

"Okay, hold your thinking for a minute," I say. "I'm putting a story written by Mark Lopez, a fifth grader, up on the overhead. You will also get a copy. Follow along as I read aloud."

I read "The Never-Ending Game" from *Our Stories*, a collection of children's fiction writing compiled by Marion Dane Bauer. The story revolves around a young boy, Alex, who steals an antique gun for a prank, then wrestles with his conscience. Students listen as I think aloud about the parts of the story that make it work.

"Hey, I *get* it!" interrupts Dawn. "There's something the same in all fiction writing, like, well, for one, the writer has to kind of paint the place where everything happens, the setting. You know, kind of use words to put a picture in our minds."

"Yeah," agrees Jake. "I can totally see that kid Alex and his loser friend Shaq, fast-pedaling from Dina's house with the stolen gun."

Tim adds, "But if a story is good, you have to see the character, too. You have to be able to kinda relate to him and he has to seem real . . . like if I were Alex I would be thinking the same things he does. I'd want to tell my Dad but I'd be afraid to, too."

Kelly leans forward in the circle and comments, "Stephen King's story does the same thing. I can totally see Trisha and feel her fear when she gets lost in the woods."

"Good thinking, guys," I comment. "So, you think character and setting are important in fiction. During workshop today, as you read, jot down more things you notice that fiction writers do. We'll share at the end. Happy hunting!"

In a fiction inquiry in Karen's classroom, students investigate the genre and list its criteria. Immersing themselves in fiction pieces, students learn first the "feel" of fiction. Karen and I pose initial questions and work with the students to discover answers. But always students' questions drive the inquiry and their noticings become the criteria for fiction writing. They move on to articulate and voice their understandings. Finally they "try on" this genre in notebooks and drafting, returning again and again to the fiction texts chosen as their models.

CHARACTERISTICS OF FICTION

Emerging writers sometimes view writing fiction as a license to describe any action, create any character, select any setting, or develop any plot, regardless of truth or reality. The temptation to produce such writing ends up in a kind of TV fiction—poor retellings of stories of favorite action-figure heroes from the world of the small screen. How do we teach students to move beyond such writing? Quite simply, we ask students to write stories, but stories from their personal experience, and we plan the unit sequentially to follow a memoir study. Writing from the center of one's experience makes a story—real or made-up—ring true. So, what makes fiction different from memoir? The starting points are the same. We draw from actual incidents in our lives, characters we know, plots we have lived through (or, at least, observed), and settings where we have worked or played. But then, we take liberties and stretch the writing to make features more vivid.

We argue that character and plot development are the two characteristics most important within the genre of fiction. William Noble writes that "characters—people—are what give a story life." We see this clearly in Katherine Paterson's *Bridge to Terabithia*. She lets us see inside Jess, the young protagonist, when she writes: *Jess drew the way some people drink whiskey. The peace would start at the top of his muddled brain and seep down through his tired and tensed-up body. Lord, he loved to draw* (p. 10). We listen to Jess's thoughts and words, creating a picture of him in our minds. In the same chapter, we meet Leslie and see her through Jess's eyes: *The person [Leslie] had jaggedy brown hair cut close to its face and wore one of those blue undershirt-like tops with faded jeans cut off above the knees* (p. 18). We anticipate what Jess and Leslie's relationship will be as we turn the pages. Although still sketchy, our picture of these characters intensifies. We are hooked. We want to know more about them. Paterson does all this brilliantly, never telling, always showing—character development at its best. In our classes, we examine skillful character development like Paterson's with our students, and use such writing as a model to follow.

A good story also has enough tension to draw the reader into the plot, questioning at each turn: What's going to happen next? In Gary Paulsen's *Hatchet*, we find a good example of such tension in chapter 8. *At first he thought it was a growl*, we read. Mystified, like the character Brian, we do not know what made that growl. Detail by detail, we learn the answer: a porcupine. A short but exquisite example of the use of tension in a plot.

EXAMPLES OF FICTION IN CHILDREN'S LITERATURE

For young writers, picture books afford the best examples of fiction writing. Donald Crews's *Shortcut* is one example of a picture book with a problem/resolution plot. Patricia Polacco's *Chicken Sunday* is another, with beautifully described characters—Eula Walker's voice, for example, "like slow thunder and sweet rain." Chapter books and novels, often used as read-alouds, provide other models of good fiction writing. Children wait breathlessly for plots to unfold in books such as Lois Lowry's *Gathering Blue* or Madeleine L'Engle's *A Wrinkle in Time*. Additional recommended fiction titles are listed in Appendix A.

TECHNIQUES WRITERS OFTEN USE IN FICTION

In moving from memoir to fiction, we focus first on developing the "sense of story" by writing from a plan. Because the problem/resolution is critical to this genre, we want students to plan their development, to describe the struggle characters face in resolving the problem. Students should think about a sequence of episodes. In some of the episodes the main character moves closer to the resolution, but in others he or she meets obstacles. Tension builds as the character struggles, fails, gets back up, and tries again until, in the final scene, the character meets with success. One first grader grasped this well in the story she wrote, shown below. She set up the problem: The alligator's tail had disappeared. What could have happened? Well, the male alligator tried to get at the female's eggs. The two alligators wrestled and the more well-equipped female did a job on that male, ripping off his tail. However, all's well that ends well. After a visit to the vet, the alligator, minus a tail, returned, sadder but wiser.

The "show, don't tell" factor is front and center in our lessons. We focus on character development most intensively in this genre. In creating each scene, we develop the characters through their thoughts, words, actions, and feelings. We emphasize the importance of specificity. We enhance dialogue by including thoughts and actions.

ALGATER AVECHER (ALLIGATOR ADVENTURE)

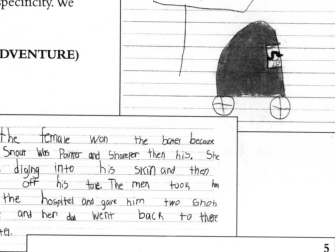

One day, Claire and her dad went to Alligator Adventure. Claire saw a lot of alligators, but before they left, one alligator's tail was gone!

They asked what happened. The man said, "Overnight that alligator got very close to some female's eggs. So the alligators wrestled."

Both of the alligators tried to win the battle. Then, the female won the battle, because her snout was pointier and sharper than his. She started digging into his skin and then tore off his tail. The men took him to the hospital and gave him two shots. Claire and her dad went back to the hotel.

 *One day Claire and her dad went to Algater Avecher. Claire sow a lot Of Aigaters but befor they left one algaters tule was gone!*

We ask what hapon. The man said Over night that Algater got very Clost to Some Females eggs. So the algaters Festuld. Both of the algaters trid to win the batel.

Then the female won the batel becauce her Snout was Poinier and Shareper then his. She Started diging into his skin and then tared off his tale. The men took him to the hospitel and gave him two shots Claire and her dad went back to there hottel.

FICTION LESSON: Writing From a Plan

Taught by Jane Sullivan in David Jackson's fifth grade class,
Upper Township Elementary School, Upper Township, New Jersey

Any carpenter knows the saying "measure twice, cut once." Seeing a story as a whole before writing saves us from wasting time. Even though our students like to plunge into draft writing, we show them that planning ahead allows them to think through the plot even before they draft. The plan also acts as a guide as they write, keeping them from straying from their goal.

PREPARATION AND MATERIALS NEEDED:

- a picture book with which students are familiar, such as Patricia Polacco's *Chicken Sunday*
- a story map of the picture book you use, written on chart paper or a transparency
- transparency of a story-map template
- copies of the blank, labeled story map for each student

STEP ONE

Review the elements of a story, using the story you've chose as a model.

PURPOSE
Discussing elements of a familiar story helps student see how an author develops the plot.

NARRATIVE
"Yesterday, we read Patricia Polacco's *Chicken Sunday*. Today, I want you to think about what a writer does when he or she starts to write a story. Let's look at *Chicken Sunday* again to find out how Patricia Polacco planned that book." I open the book and read the first sentence: *Stewart and Winston were my neighbors.*

"What do we learn from that sentence?"

Philip raises his hand. "The characters' names?"

"Hmmm," I answer. "Are you saying that we need characters in a story?"

He nods.

"Okay, so characters are one part of what we call the story map." I write the word *characters* on the chart. "What we are writing here is the story map of *Chicken Sunday*." Below the heading "Characters," I write "Stewart, Winston."

STORY MAP OF CHICKEN SUNDAY

Characters
Stewart, Winston

Setting (Time, Place)
small town in the 1940's

Problem
Wanted to buy a hat

Plot

threw the eggs--

decorated the eggs--

sold the eggs

Resolution
raised the money

Teaching the Elements of Powerful Writing

STEP TWO

Leave a space below "Characters" (later, we will insert "Setting" here). Talk about how the author introduced the problem as the beginning of the plot of a story.

PURPOSE

After characters, problem is the next major element in a story. Setting can be explained later (see step 6).

NARRATIVE

"What else?" I ask.

"You need stuff happening," says Amanda.

"Okay," I say, writing "plot" on the chart. "We call the 'stuff' that happens the *plot*. There is something very important in the plot of a good story. Listen to this line and see whether someone can tell me what is going on." I read: *We wanted to get her that hat more than anything in the world.* "Let's think about that sentence. It tells us a lot about this story, doesn't it?"

Michael's hand comes up slowly. "They wanted to get her the hat but they didn't have enough money."

"That's a smart answer, Michael," I say. "They had a problem, didn't they?" I write "Problem" on the chart. Below it I write: "wanted to buy a hat."

STEP THREE

Discuss how the struggle to solve the problem leads to the resolution.

PURPOSE

Students need to recognize that the plot involves resolving the problem through a struggle.

NARRATIVE

"So, what did they have to do?" I ask.

Michael continues. "They had to think of a way to get the money to buy the hat."

Britney pops up. "But then, they got into trouble. Mr.—ohhh, I forget his name—thought they threw the eggs."

Now Lexis helps out. "Mr. Kodinski," she says. "But the eggs gave them the idea of decorating eggs. So that's how they got the money."

"You are all so smart," I say, writing the resolution—"raised the money"—under "Problem" but with enough space between the two words to add the steps in reaching the resolution. "They solved the problem." I point to the word *resolution*. "We call that a resolution. Almost like the solution in math."

STEP FOUR

Emphasize the importance of struggle in a fiction story.

PURPOSE

Students need to know that the story evolves through tension and struggle.

NARRATIVE

I say, "Now, another question. Was it easy for them to do all that?"

A chorus of "no's" tells me the group is in agreement.

"You're right. The three children in the story had to struggle to get the answer to their problem." I acknowledge, and write "STRUGGLE" in capital letters in the margin between problem and resolution. Then I write: "threw the eggs—decorated the eggs—sold the eggs" underneath.

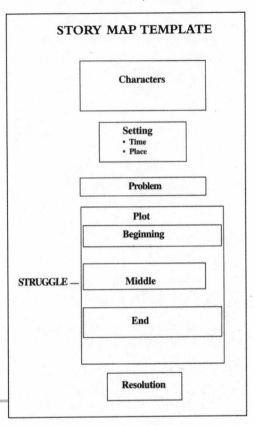

Review the major elements found in a story.

PURPOSE

Reviewing the complete structure helps student see it as a whole.

NARRATIVE

"Okay," I say. "Let's look at what we have here. A story must have . . . ?"

I point to the word *characters* and pause to let students respond.

"Characters."

I continue, pausing each time for their response. "It needs a . . . ?"

"Plot"

"Now, the plot starts with a . . . ?"

"Problem."

"There is a . . . ?"

"Struggle."

"Until finally we come to a . . ."

"Resolution."

STORY MAP TEMPLATE

Characters

Setting
• Time
• Place

Problem

Plot

Beginning

STRUGGLE — Middle

End

Resolution

Allow students to discover the missing setting—or call their attention to it yourself.

PURPOSE

Letting students discover the blank space in the completed story map invites interaction.

NARRATIVE

I put up a transparency with a story map template. "Here's what we just discussed," I say. "I prepared this last night. What do you think?"

Jesse raises his hand. "What's setting?" he asks.

"Sharp eyes, Jesse," I say. "We didn't talk about that, did we?"

Steve calls out, "I think it's where the story is happening."

"Where did *Chicken Sunday* happen?" I ask.

"It didn't say," Steve answers.

"Can we guess?" I ask.

Jesse thinks a bit. "It could have happened in a little town some-where. Like Marmora."

"But look at how people are dressed," says Britney. "Not like now."

I nod. "Okay, but when?"

"Maybe back when Miss Polacco was a girl?" she says.

"That's a good guess," I answer. "I would say around the forties or the fifties." On the transparency of the *Chicken Sunday* story map, I write: "Setting (time, place): small town in the 1940s."

STEP SEVEN

Clarify students' use of setting.

PURPOSE
Students need to be aware of the settings they will use in their stories.

NARRATIVE

When will your stories take place?"

"Now," Britney answers.

I write that in the space. "And where?"

"Marmora."

"Seaville."

"Tuckahoe." Answers come from all corners of the room.

"Maine," says Cody.

"If you've been there, you can use it in your story," I respond.

STEP EIGHT

Using the labeled copy of the story map, discuss its usefulness.

PURPOSE
Students need to discover the purpose of an outline and why they should use one.

NARRATIVE

I ask Amanda to give out copies of a labeled story map and return my copy to the overhead. "We can use an outline like this to plan our story. How will this help us, do you think?" I ask.

Miles takes a guess. "It will keep us on track?"

I smile. It's something I say often—stay on track. "That surely will help," I agree. "What else?"

Harley tries. "Maybe, it saves us time. We don't have to go back and change things and cross out a lot when we write it?"

"Sure," I say. "We can make sure our story will work. If we need to make a change, we can do it on the outline."

STEP NINE

Send students off to begin the outline of the story they will write.

PURPOSE
Having students map out their story allows us to check on the strength of their piece before they put time into drafting it.

NARRATIVE

"Now you need to think about your story. Let's get to work. Fill in the spaces of your story map with the idea you have for your story."

The students take various positions. Some begin writing vigorously; others glance out the window, thinking. I move from table to table, advising, encouraging, and listening. The project has begun.

MAKING REVISIONS EASIER

Students work on their outlines individually, then confer with me or with their partner. Below is Cody's story map. After our conference, he added an episode to his plot (see addition in the story map's margin) to build up the

struggle. From this experience, Cody learned an easier way to revise, and changed his written draft accordingly.

FOR YOUNGER CHILDREN

While the story map as an outline has been used successfully even in first grade, the mentor text used as a model should have a simple plot structure, appropriate for the grade level.

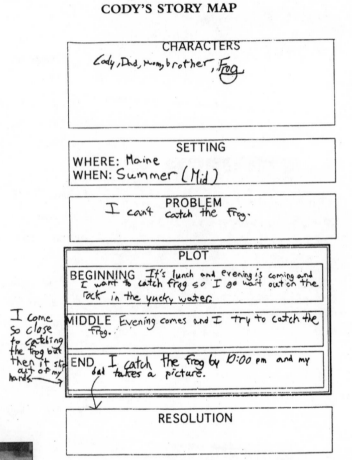

CODY'S STORY MAP

CHARACTERS
Cody, Dad, Mom, brother, Frog.

SETTING
WHERE: Maine
WHEN: Summer (Mid)

PROBLEM
I can't catch the Frog.

PLOT

BEGINNING It's lunch and evening is coming and I want to catch frog so I go wait out on the rock in the yucky water.

MIDDLE Evening comes and I try to catch the frog.

I come so close to catching the frog but then it slip out of my hands.

END, I catch the frog by 10:00 pm and my dad takes a picture.

RESOLUTION

FICTION LESSON: Seeing the Scene

Taught by Midge Madden in Kathy Carhart's fifth grade class,
William Winchester Elementary School, Westminster, Maryland

In *What a Writer Needs*, Ralph Fletcher argues that the setting creates the world in which characters live and grapple with problems and conflict. Readers stick with writing that hooks them into an intriguing, and usually believable, world; they read and connect with sensory language that lets them visualize the place where story action unfolds.

But we have found that, in describing the scenes in the stories they write, young writers often omit important details, frequently using one-liners such as "in my grandma's kitchen" or "when we arrived at Disney World." We need to show students that *seeing* the scene in our writer's mind and *setting* the scene for the reader's eye are important elements of writing good fiction.

We begin by helping them to use their five senses in describing a place or scene. We also show them how to add detail to build a vivid mind-picture.

PREPARATION AND MATERIALS NEEDED:

- writer's notebooks
- a blank chart
- transparencies of two teacher writing samples
- sketching paper
- colored markers

STEP ONE

Tell students that writers invite readers into their story worlds by using sensory language to evoke images in their readers' minds.

PURPOSE
Students learn that rich detail and description are important elements of good fiction writing.

NARRATIVE
"I've been working a lot lately in my writing to make my scenes—the setting or places about which I write—'come alive,'" I say. "Sometimes it is really hard to show my readers what a scene in my story looks like, especially because as a writer I can only use words. So today I'm going to share a piece I've been working on. Tell me what you notice."

STEP TWO

Put a piece of your writing on the overhead and read it aloud.

PURPOSE
Students will see and hear a written description of a setting.

NARRATIVE

"Okay, listen up. I'm going to read a piece of writing to you," I say. "As I read, I want you to jot down whatever you notice about this writing. When I'm finished, we'll talk about your noticings."

Jared puts his hand up. "What should we be looking for?" he asks.

"What do you notice about the writing that makes it come alive for you?" I ask. I read my piece of writing.

SEEING THE SCENE: MODEL DESCRIPTIVE TEXT

Midge Madden

The William Winchester Elementary School, affectionately known as "Willie," greets visitors with an openness that says, "Welcome. We're glad you're here." Two brightly colored roadrunner mats—the roadrunner is the school's mascot—prompt a smile. In the wide, sunny foyer, sparkling floors, freshly painted walls and a huge "Willie" tree invite guests to view photos of the Willie family.

Chris Sparr, the vice-principal and Mark Vigliotti, the principal, immediately provide welcome, direction, and assistance. Janet Albaugh and Linda Bach, who man the main office with efficiency and calmness, greet me with friendly smiles, snap my picture for a new Willie ID, and print out a map and faculty directory for me. Hurrying through the office, Rose Phillips gives an enthusiastic wave. The librarian, Jenny, mouths "welcome" as she makes an announcement over the loudspeaker about unclaimed library books. It seems indeed a happy place; adults move with purpose but with camaraderie as well. "Where are the kids?" I wonder, noticing only a few well-behaved children in the cafeteria. "Oh, they don't come in until nine," Janet informs me.

As if on cue, the halls fill with children who purposefully head to their hallway lockers, stow their backpacks and lunches, and enter classrooms. "Hi, Mrs. Strine," smiles Natalie. "Are we doing author study today?" "This afternoon, Nat," Mrs. Strine promises. Five-year-old Heaven pulls her mother towards the all-day kindergarten room. "C'mon, Mommy. I'll be late for read-aloud!" Mark Vigliotti's voice welcomes, "Good Morning," and "God Bless America" booms over the loudspeaker. I watch as stragglers drop book bags and stand with hands over hearts, pledging allegiance to the flag.

STEP THREE

Have students share their noticings about how you create a setting or scene.

PURPOSE

Students learn about writing by making and sharing observations about model texts.

NARRATIVE

I chart students' noticings under the heading, "Setting the Scene." "What did you notice about my scene?" I ask.

Jared volunteers, "You used lots of descriptive words like 'sunny foyer' and 'sparkling floors.' I could easily see what the school's hallways looked like."

Sharon chimed in, "Yeah, but you also used talk, I mean, you had the actual words that people say. That makes me feel like I'm listening and hearing teachers talk, too. You know, I really feel like I'm there at Willie!" Sharon smiles.

"What else?" I ask.

Joel slowly raises his hand. "Well . . . I don't know quite how to explain it, but I kinda felt like I was moving around with you. . . . I felt the action, I guess."

Alex seconds, saying, "Yeah, like when the librarian whispered welcome, I could see her lips moving. And I could see all the kids coming into school and pledging the allegiance."

"Great job!" I say. "Now I want you to try something on your own."

SEEING THE SCENE

Noticings about "William Winchester" portrait

WHAT WE NOTICED:

1. Lots of descriptive phrases like "sunny foyer" and "sparkling floors"

2. Use of talk or dialogue to help us see the characters

3. Characters move in the scene; readers sense action

4. Lots of detail; spent a whole paragraph describing the main hallway of the school

---

Distribute a photocopy of a second piece of writing that describes a scene.

PURPOSE
Students need to try out new learning; working with a partner helps to lessen feelings of uncertainty and encourages risk-taking.

NARRATIVE
I say, "I'm going to give you and your writing partner a piece of text to read together and analyze. Ask one another, 'Is this a good example of a text that creates a picture in your mind?' If so, what makes you think this?"

SEEING THE SCENE: MODEL DESCRIPTIVE TEXT
Midge Madden

They had been walking for days, stalker and stalked. They watched for signs . . . trampled undergrowth, even a possible footprint. They listened to the silence of the woods. Nothing. Discouraged and exhausted, the two trekkers collapsed onto a decayed, broken log.

"You know, Pete, I'm beginning to get spooked. He's got to be out here somewhere, but dang if I know where else to look. I'm beginning to feel like he's tracking us!"

Intent yellow eyes flecked with red stared from the dense underbrush a few feet from the men. The lion. He stood motionless, his massive frame hidden by forest and early morning mist. He snarled softly, baring huge teeth, then slowly backed away.

Oblivious to the nearby danger, the two men shook off their fatigue and hoisted their packs onto their backs. Pete carried the rifle, while Jake slung the crossbow over his shoulder.

The mountain lion snarled again.

"Did ya har that?" Pete whispered. "Hang on a minute. I'm going up the tree for a look."

Suddenly the lion attacked. Crashing through the underbrush, he charged the oak and began to climb.

WHOOSH! The arrow flew through the mist.

"Jake!" Pete cried.

The lion climbed steadily, reaching the limb to which Pete clung. Pulling the crossbow, Jake aimed again. WHOOSH! This time the arrow hit its mark, lodging in the lion's heart. Blood spurted from the wound. Enraged, the lion swiped his heavy paw, narrowly missing Pete. His jaws snapped, eyes wide in surprised disbelief. Blood soaked his massive chest, coloring his fur crimson. Crazed with pain, the lion swung again wildly, then toppled backwards to the ground with a thunderous crash.

Ask students to listen to the sensory language they find and create mental pictures. Then, have them draw these mental images and share their visual interpretations.

PURPOSE

Drawing interpretations of written scenes helps to make descriptive writing concrete for young writers. Students learn that careful choice of words results in vivid scene writing that enables readers to make pictures in their minds.

NARRATIVE

I say, "Working as partners, I'd like one of you to read the writing quietly and the other to close his or her eyes. Then switch. After you finish, each of you sketches what you see in your mind."

I walk around the classroom as students huddle in twos, reading quietly and then sketching. I listen to Alex and Sam whisper to one another.

"Here's what I see happening," suggests Alex. "But it's kinda confusing, don't you think? I mean the writing is . . . "

Nodding, Sam adds, "Yeah, pretty confusing. But I think drawing the scene helps me to understand. Do we have the same idea in our sketches?"

The two boys compare their drawings and smile. "Yep!"

I smile, too, and ask partners to share with the whole group. Alex offers to explain his sketched interpretation.

I hear murmurs of agreement—"Hey, I saw the same thing!"—as well as "aha!" moments for some—"So, that's what's happening! I couldn't figure out who was in the tree!"

ALEX'S SKETCH

STEP SIX

Have students return to the mentor text and mark up words that helped them to create mental images. Put the mentor text on the overhead.

PURPOSE
Students need to be able to recognize descriptive language and word images that conjure up mind pictures.

NARRATIVE

"Okay, everyone. Let's see what we did." I direct the class's attention to the writing on the overhead. "Who would like to volunteer to mark up the text and show some 'mind picture' words?" I ask.

Different students come forward and circle phrases on the transparency that help them to "see" the scene.

MARKED-UP TEXT SHOWING WORDS THAT CONJURED UP IMAGES

They had been walking for days, stalker and stalked. They watched for signs … trampled undergrowth, even a possible footprint. They listened to the silence of the woods. Nothing. Discouraged and exhausted, the two trekkers collapsed onto a decayed, broken log.

"You know, Pete, I'm beginning to get spooked. He's got to be out here somewhere, but dang if I know where else to look. I'm beginning to feel like he's tracking *us!*"

Intent yellow eyes flecked with red stared from the dense underbrush a few feet from the men. The lion. He stood motionless, his massive frame hidden by forest and early morning mist. He snarled softly, baring huge teeth, then slowly backed away.

Oblivious to the near danger, the two men shook off their fatigue and hoisted their packs back onto their backs. Pete carried the rifle, while Jake slung the crossbow over his shoulder.

The mountain lion snarled again.

"Did ya hear that?" Pete whispered. "Hang on a minute. I'm going up the tree for a look."
Pete scrambled up the towering oak, leaving his rifle below.

Suddenly the lion attacked. Crashing through the underbrush, he charged the oak and began to climb.

WHOOSH! The arrow flew through the mist.

"JAKE!" Pete cried.

The lion climbed steadily, reaching the limb to which Pete clung. Pulling the crossbow, Jake aimed again. WHOOSH! This time the arrow hit its mark, lodging in the lion's heart. Blood spurted from the wound. Enraged, the lion swiped his heavy paw, narrowly missing Pete. His jaws snapped wide, eyes wide in surprised disbelief. Blood soaked his massive chest, coloring his fur crimson red. Crazed with pain, the lion swung again wildly, then toppled backwards to the ground with a thunderous crash.

DEVELOPING VIVID SCENES

Students work independently to try writing their own scenes. We talk about adding detail, using dialogue, searching for descriptive words and vivid images, and trying to make the characters move within the setting. As Georgia Heard suggests in *The Revision Toolbox*, we help young writers to use words that will create movies in the mind.

FOR YOUNGER CHILDREN

With second and third graders, use a simpler text as a model. Read the text aloud and have a volunteer demonstrate, role-playing the action in slow motion. Display a copy of the mentor text on overhead. Invite students to come up and circle the mind-picture words they see in the text.

FICTION LESSON: Stretching the Moment

Created by Karen Flagg, and taught to her fifth grade class at P.S. 242, New York City

We teach and help students to discover that good fiction often "stretches the moment" or tells a lot about one small moment in time. This technique can create tension in a story *and* draw the reader in. It puts the reader in the scene, slows down the action of the plot, and holds the attention of the reader.

When student writers develop plots, they often "fly by" or hurdle over critical moments that are pivotal to the story—moments that, if developed, would *be* the story. Students often get to the end too quickly, as does Dale, who writes: *It was the first time I hit a baseball. We won the game. It was a lot of fun.*

But when teachers model how stretching a moment builds tension in writing, writing such as Dale's can change to:

> *It was my up at bat. I stood nervously at home plate. The pitcher released the ball from his hand. I saw the ball come towards me. I moved to swing the bat. All I heard was "clink." It hit the gate. I made it safe to first base. The man on third scored the winning run.*

We must teach students to differentiate here. What *is* the more interesting story and *why*? Teachers can use texts such as Roald Dahl's *Boy* or Karen Hesse's *Come On, Rain* to demonstrate this writing strategy.

PREPARATION AND MATERIALS NEEDED:

- transparencies of two samples of teacher writing
- black transparency marker
- students' writing notebooks
- chart paper
- a book such as *Come On, Rain* by Karen Hesse

STEP ONE

Introduce the strategy of stretching the moment.

PURPOSE
Students need to recognize this strategy as a way to enhance writing.

NARRATIVE
"Have you ever been on a roller coaster?" Karen asks. "Think about what it's like when you're just about to reach the summit. Doesn't it feel like forever before you go screaming downhill? Your stomach is in your throat, your heart is pounding like mad, and you're looking at all of these little bodies down below waving their arms frantically, but you can't hear a sound. You hear the last two clicks as the car lurches over the hill and you say to yourself, 'Please, will I make it to the end of this ride in one piece?' Then, suddenly, the car goes roaring downhill and you can't get the smile off of your face! Well, authors make you feel this way through their writing. They are really able to stretch the moment."

STEP TWO

Show a piece of teacher writing on the overhead and choose a sentence in that piece to "stretch the moment" by adding more details.

PURPOSE

Students will see how to go back into a piece of their writing and select a moment to stretch, i.e., add more details.

NARRATIVE

Karen puts her first writing sample on the overhead. Students read it silently while she thinks aloud. "The climax of the story is not when I hit the ball but when the ball crashed through Mrs. Reynolds's window. I think my piece would be so much better if I really stretch the part when the ball went through the window. I'm going to stretch out that moment: *'Whack!* I hit the ball hard and it went right through Mrs. Reynolds's window,'" she says. "Watch me."

> **KAREN'S FIRST SAMPLE**
>
> It was my turn up at bat. I remembered what my father told me. Keep your eye on the ball, choke up on the bat, and swing through. I was ready. "Sink in," shouted the older kids. I'll show them, I thought to myself. Artie okayed the pitch. He wound up and released a fastball aimed straight over home plate. "I can do this!" I thought to myself. *Whack!* I hit the ball hard and it smashed into Mrs. Reynolds's window.

STEP THREE

Rewrite the line on a new transparency as you do a "think-aloud," i.e., express thoughts about the moment out loud.

PURPOSE

The think-aloud allows students to "see" the mental processes of a more proficient writer.

NARRATIVE

Karen rewrites the sentence on a new transparency, while thinking aloud. "I remember that everything seemed to be in slow motion. I knew the other kids thought I hit like a girl. I was going to show them. Shouts from my team erupted, 'W-H-O-AA!' I smiled and I knew that the older kids were impressed. The ball went sailing over the fire hydrant, our third base. I let go of the bat with my left hand and headed towards first base. The ball was still high in the sky as I rounded second. I grinned as I ran towards third. Suddenly Danny hollered, 'Oh, no!' I looked around at the other players who seemed to be frozen solid. They had terrified looks on their faces. *Smash!* My ball went right through Mrs. Reynolds's window."

KAREN'S STRETCHING THE MOMENT

It was my turn up at bat. I remembered what my father told me. Keep your eye on the ball, choke up on the bat, and swing through. I was ready. "Sink in," shouted the older kids. I'll show them, I thought to myself. Artie okayed the pitch. He wound up and released a fastball aimed straight over home plate. "I can do this!" I thought to myself. *Whack!*

I remember that everything seemed to be in slow motion. I knew the other kids thought I hit like a girl. I was going to show them. Shouts from my team erupted, "W-H-O-AA!" I smiled and I knew that the older kids were impressed. The ball went sailing over the fire hydrant, our third base. I let go of the bat with my left hand and headed towards first base. The ball was still high in the sky as I rounded second. I grinned and ran towards third. Suddenly Danny hollered, "Oh, no!" I looked around at the other players who seemed to be frozen solid. They had terrified looks on their faces. *Smash!* My ball went right through Mrs. Reynolds's window.

STEP FOUR

Ask the students what they notice about your stretched writing.

PURPOSE
Students need opportunities to study revised writing and to articulate why the revised text is better, and in this particular lesson, why adding descriptive details improves a piece of writing.

NARRATIVE

"What do you notice about this piece of writing?" Karen asks.

"Well . . . I can see the scene in my mind a whole lot better," begins Annie.

"Yeah," Jared jumps in. "You added so much detail—you actually wrote a whole paragraph from that one sentence. And you used talk, I mean dialogue. That makes it seem so real somehow."

Karen nods. "Anything else?"

Sarah speaks softly from the back. "It feels like you just wrote the scene in slow motion, kinda like instant replay. The words you use and the way you build up to the final moment when she breaks the window are really good. But I don't think I can do that kind of writing."

Karen counters, "Why, sure you can, Sarah. Let's take a moment to review and chart all that we have noticed."

Students work with Karen to list their noticings.

STUDENTS' NOTICINGS

- added details
- used dialogue
- wrote in slow motion

STEP FIVE

Have students select a sentence from their own writing and stretch the moment.

PURPOSE

When students can apply new knowledge to their own writing, they understand the technique being taught.

NARRATIVE

"Now it's your turn to try and stretch a moment in your writing," Karen encourages. "Off you go. I'll be around to see how you're doing."

MAKING A DIFFERENCE

At this point, students work independently, following Karen's model. They select a moment to stretch from their personal stories, write the sentence at the top of their notebook page, and begin. Karen circles the room, noticing students' work. She takes note of techniques being used. The ones she sees and hears repeatedly: using dialogue, talking about feelings at that particular moment, talking in their heads out loud, and using people's names.

At the end of the writing workshop, the students gather in the meeting area. Karen asks, "How did it feel?"

Kristoffer comments, "It wasn't that easy, but it really made my story better."

Lucy adds, "Yeah, a lot better!"

Karen nods, "So we all agree that stretching a moment really makes a difference in our writing? Who would like to share?"

Karen selects three volunteers to read their initial lines and their new and improved stretched moments aloud.

> Ariel
> January 9
>
> It was the first day of school and I didn't know how jump double dutch Plus I never tried it. Brianna said just try it and so did Brandi. They started turning back and fourth, back and fourth. I started jumping in. I could hear the click click, click click of the rope. I tried to get the rhythem of the rope. I jumped in and I did pretty well. The whistle blew and we tried to get our last jump but we couldn't.

> Dale
> ~~It was the first time I hit a baseball~~
> I saw the ball come towards me.
> I moved to swing the bat.
> All I heard was clink.
> It hit the gate.
> I made it safe to first base.

FOR YOUNGER CHILDREN

For grades two and three, the teacher might draw out children's responses with prompts like "And then what happened?" or "How did that make you feel?" or "What did you do?" or "What did you say?"

Teaching the Elements of Powerful Writing

FICTION LESSON: Creating Characters From the Inside Out

Created by Karen Flagg, and taught to her fifth grade class at P.S. 242, New York City

As readers, we often make instant connections with characters in stories, usually because they remind us of people we know. We sympathize with Charlie Bucket in his search to find the golden ticket, only to discover chocolate. We shudder with Stanley Yelnats as he enters Camp Green Lake and faces the imminent dangers of yellow-spotted lizards. And we smile when Annie and Clover sit side by side on the fence, pushing aside the fears of their mothers. Authors such as Roald Dahl, Louis Sachar, and Jacqueline Woodson hook us into their stories by creating believable characters that touch our hearts. We *feel* with the characters, often putting ourselves in their places to overcome their struggle. As readers, we get to know characters very well from the inside out. But the writing? The how-to? Creating believable characters is much more difficult to achieve.

This lesson suggests a way to teach students how to create three-dimensional characters in their fiction writing.

PREPARATION AND MATERIALS NEEDED:

- a novel such as *Journey* by Patricia MacLachlan
- Outside/Inside T-Chart
- blank transparency or chart paper
- writer's notebooks

STEP ONE

Ask students to define you as a character.

PURPOSE

We need to help students understand how character development includes more than simple description of outward appearance. Using a concrete example (e.g., yourself) helps students understand ways to develop characters in their writing.

NARRATIVE

Karen begins, "So many of the characters that we read about in books often remind us of people we know in the real world. We get to know characters very well from the inside out. Authors show us what characters are thinking and feeling as well as what they look like. Think for a moment. If I was going to be a character in a story, what could you say about me? What am I like on the outside? What am I like on the inside?"

STEP TWO

List different character traits that students generate about you from the inside and outside.

PURPOSE
We chart this so that students can visualize a way to generate inside and outside traits about a person/character.

NARRATIVE

Karen directs students' attention to a T-chart she has prepared. The left-hand column is headed: "Outside," the right-hand column: "Inside."

"Look at me. What do you notice on the outside? What types of traits can we list?" Karen jots down ideas that students share. "Great. These noticings are what you see when you look at me from the outside. But, you guys *know* me. You know a lot about me. What can you say about who I am on the inside?"

Students think and offer ideas. Karen writes their thoughts down under the "inside" column.

Outside/Inside Chart of Karen	
Outside	**Inside**
Long blonde hair	Nice because she reads us books
Greenish eyes	Knowledgeable --knows lots of stuff
Lots of moles or beauty marks	Honest and expects us to tell the truth
Thin	Loves her family because she always talks about them and shows photos
black pants	
Black V-neck sweater	
Wears fun socks	

STEP THREE

Have students listen as you read the first chapter of a selected novel. (We use *Journey* by Patricia MacLachlan, but many novels work well here.)

PURPOSE
Students need to understand that good writers show the outside and the inside of the characters they create.

NARRATIVE

Karen says, "Now let's think about a fictional character. For example, take the main character, Journey, in Patricia MacLachlan's book. Even though we've just begun to read it, let's try to understand what we already know about him. What does the author, Patricia MacLachlan, tell us? Listen again as I read Chapter One and look for clues about who Journey really is. Jot down ideas if you wish. Then let's see if we can make a list together."

STEP FOUR

Reread the chapter. Discuss and chart what students know about the outside of the character.

PURPOSE

Students need to understand that good writers develop characters by describing external features (the "outside").

NARRATIVE

Karen says, "So what do we know about Journey on the outside? I'll start. Two things I know are that Journey is a boy and he's eleven."

Jared adds, "Yeah, and his mother left, packed a suitcase, and said she'd send money."

Other students add to the list: he lives with his grandparents and a sister; he doesn't want to take pictures. Karen draws a second Outside/Inside Chart. Under the "Outside" column, she writes these items.

STEP FIVE

Turn now to information about the character's thoughts.

PURPOSE

Students should discover how a writer reveals the "inside" of a character.

NARRATIVE

Karen continues, this time using the "Inside" column of the T-chart. "So what do we know about Journey's inside?"

Josh offers, "Remember that line about Journey looking into the camera 'with such fury?' I think he seems angry."

Sarah adds, "Well, I think he is sad that his mom left."

As Karen writes their thinking on the chart, Josh chimes in, "Yeah, and he's confused, too. He's trying to figure out why she left and where she went. And I think he's kinda annoyed at his grandfather. He doesn't get why he's taking all the pictures and he thinks it's stupid."

"Good," Karen agrees, then says, "Well, I think one more thing. I think he secretly wants to understand his mother, his father, his grandmother and his grandfather. I think he's wondering who people really are on the inside."

STEP SIX

Review students' discoveries.

PURPOSE

Students need time to absorb and understand new learning. Pausing to review ideas generated and charted so far helps students better understand and provides opportunities for further questions.

NARRATIVE

Karen rereads what they have charted about the inside and outside of Journey (see right). She says, "You can see what we already

Outside/Inside Chart of Journey	
Outside	**Inside**
Eleven -year-old boy His mother left him Lives with grandparents Has an older sister, Cat Lives on a farm Hates cameras	Hurt beause his mom left angry --looks mad i picture confused, doesn't know why his mom left annoyed at his father who keeps takig what Journey calls stupid pictures

know about Journey. And if we continued to search in the story, our chart and our understanding of Journey would grow."

STEP SEVEN

Have students use inside/outside charts to brainstorm with a classmate about a fictional character that they will create.

PURPOSE

Talk helps students begin to think about ideas.

NARRATIVE

Karen says, "Now we're going to try to begin creating a character of our own. Turn to a neighbor and talk about some inside and outside character traits that might describe a character you make up."

Students turn to one another and talk about possible traits for their characters. Karen listens in to their conversations.

"GROWING" CHARACTERS

"Now it's your turn," Karen says. "You're going to fill out an Outside/Inside Chart in your notebook of your character's traits just as we did together. But this time, it's your character and you're making it up."

Students return to their tables, draw the T-chart in their notebooks and make lists. Karen circulates, asks questions, and gives support where needed. Then students share their ideas, talking quietly in pairs.

After ten minutes, Karen asks, "How did it go?" Jared and Sarah wave hands wildly. Karen laughs and says, "Go ahead, you two. Share your characters with the rest of us."

Sarah begins. "I created a lady named Ms. Rubin. She's a teacher who wears lots of cool jewelry and has blonde curly hair. That's her outside. But she's beautiful on the inside, too, because she gives us warnings so we won't get in trouble. And she likes all the children—no favorites!"

"Good job," says Karen. She reviews how writers create characters from the inside out. The class also begins an ongoing chart documenting what they are learning about creating characters.

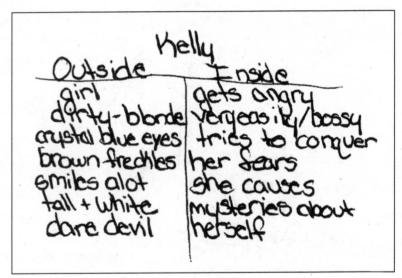

FOR YOUNGER CHILDREN

This lesson may be used in grades 2–5 with an age-appropriate text as the mentor text. Have students develop an Outside/Inside Chart with the teacher and then write from that chart.

FICTION LESSON: Color-Coding Dialogue

*Created by Sherri Brecker, and taught to her fourth grade class at
Holly Heights Elementary School, Westhampton, New Jersey*

A question many young writers wrestle with in writing dialogue is "How do we set it up?" This lesson guides students through an inquiry that helps them discover the answer to that question. Using colored markers to distinguish the parts, students learn the format for combining dialogue with name tags.

PREPARATION AND MATERIALS NEEDED:

- red and blue crayons or markers for each student
- a set of red and blue transparency markers
- a transparency and individual copies of a page of dialogue from a book students are reading, such as Karen Hesse's *A Collar for Sable*
- a chart that defines the following terms: quotation, quotation marks, name tag, and split quotation

STEP ONE

Distribute copies of the page of dialogue (see page 68). Read the text aloud.

PURPOSE
Students need to read the text first to understand what it is they will analyze.

NARRATIVE

After distributing the handouts of the page of dialogue, Sherri begins the lesson. "We've been reading Karen Hesse's book, *A Collar for Sable*," she says, placing the page of dialogue on the overhead. "Today, I'd like us to study the way authors such as Karen Hesse write dialogue. So, take your handout and let's reread this page from the book. I'll read it aloud and you follow along like readers." She reads the short excerpt aloud. The words are familiar to the students because they read this part just yesterday.

Excerpt from *A Collar for Sable* by Karen Hesse

Except for her being so skinny, Sable unfolded into a good-sized dog. She leaned against me, standing in the doorway to Pap's shop.

"If you're coming in, get on with it, Tate," Pap said. "You're letting the heat out."

I nudged Sable inside, shutting the door behind me.

Pap builds furniture for people who live in places like Boston and Hartford.

I wished Pap would let me work along with him. He never did. Pap said, "Ten is too young to work with saws and things. Besides, girls have plenty other jobs to do without messing with wood." My stomach always tightened when Pap said stuff like that.

I knelt beside Sable, stroking her all over, getting to know her with my hands. "How come Mam doesn't like dogs?" I asked.

Pap shrugged. He held a pencil between his teeth as he sighted down a piece of white oak.

Pap made a mark on the wood with the pencil. "Mam got herself tore up by a dog when she was a girl," he said. "You've seen that scar on her leg, Tate."

"I didn't know that was from a dog," I said. Mam always wore dresses that hid the scar. She didn't even like me seeing it.

The shop smell tingled inside my nose, like a sneeze coming. I wiggled my nostrils in and out, trying to get the tickle to settle down.

"She was younger than you when it happened. . . ."

STEP TWO

If the example you use is written from the first-person point of view, clarify that fact at the beginning of the inquiry.

PURPOSE

To follow the plot of a story, students need to determine the role of the narrator.

NARRATIVE

Sherri pauses. "So, who did we decide is telling this story? Who is the narrator?" She asks.

"I know," says Mark, waving his hand, "Tate."

"Find a place where Tate is speaking, Mark, and read it out loud for us," Sherri directs.

Mark runs his finger down the page. He finds the line and reads: *"How come Mam doesn't like dogs?" I asked.*

"So, when Tate is speaking, do we see Tate's name there?"

Mark shakes his head. "No, it says *I.*"

Sherri smiles. "Remember that," she says. "We'll come back to that in a little while."

STEP THREE

Using a different-colored pen for each character's name, write the character names on a white board or transparency. (In this example, we used blue for Pap and red for Tate.)

PURPOSE

Students should connect each color to a specific character. This will prove useful later in the lesson.

NARRATIVE

"Now, let's put on our writer's cap, and look at this page again," Sherri says, picking up a red marker. "Who are the two characters in the story?" Stacey's hand goes up first. "Tate and Pap," she answers. Sherri writes the two names on the white board—*Tate* in red and *Pap* in blue.

STEP FOUR

Write an example of a line of dialogue and review the terminology: quotation, quotation marks, name tag. Call students' attention to the chart on dialogue parts, created in a previous lesson.

PURPOSE
A review of the terminology brings prior knowledge to the forefront, readying students for the application.

NARRATIVE

On the board, Sherri writes: "'I have a dog and his name is Bingo,' I said."

"Now, let's review what we know about writing dialogue," she says. "What do we call the part I underlined? If you don't know, look at the dialogue chart."

Glancing at the chart hanging on the bulletin board, Mark answers, "Quotation."

"Good, Mark," she says. "You remembered to look for the clues." Over the underlined words Sherri writes, "Quotation."

"What are these?" she asks, pointing to the quotation marks.

Heads turn to the chart for the answer. "Quotation marks," says Drew.

Sherri writes that above each pair, then points to *I said* and asks, "Who can see what we call this?"

Tim finds this answer. "Name tag," he says. Sherri writes that above the two name-tag words.

PARTS OF DIALOGUE

"I like my dog," I said. (Quotation)

"I like my dog," I said. (Quotation marks)

"I like my dog," I said. (Name tag)

"My dog chews my slippers," I said, "but I still like him." (Split quotation)

STEP FIVE

Have students locate a line of dialogue in their handouts of the text. Students should help peers who cannot find the dialogue in question.

PURPOSE
Students helping one another promotes and/or reinforces learning for each.

NARRATIVE

"Now," Sherri continues, "let's look at this page from our book again. Put your finger on the first place where Tate speaks. The line of dialogue is at the very bottom of the page. Show the person next to you, if he or she needs help," she reminds them, checking quickly to see that everyone has found that line. "What are Tate's words?"

STEP SIX

Prompt students to notice how the quotation marks are placed in the example.

PURPOSE

In an inquiry, it is important that students discover for themselves; teachers provide the necessary coaching.

NARRATIVE

Tim reads: "'*How come Mam doesn't like dogs?*'"

"Good job, Tim," Sherri responds. "You found what Tate said. But how did you know those were her words?"

Tim doesn't have an answer, so Sherri prompts him. "How do we know someone is speaking? What punctuation is there?"

Kim's hand goes up. "The quotes that go around it."

"Yes," Sherri says.

STEP SEVEN

Have students identify where the question mark used in the quotation is placed. Show students how to distinguish speakers by underlining a character's spoken words (quotation) consistently in the same color. In this case, Tate's are in red.

PURPOSE

Using this color-coding technique helps students visualize the structure we use when writing dialogue.

NARRATIVE

Sherri continues to model questions we ask in an inquiry. Students respond well. "What is the first word Tate said, Kim?"

"*How.*"

"And the last?"

"*Dogs.*"

"And is the question mark inside or outside of the quotation marks?"

A chorus of voices answers. "Inside."

Sherri underlines: *How come Mam doesn't like dogs?* in red on the transparency. "Underline those words on your copy in red," she says.

STEP EIGHT

Students find another example of dialogue from the same character.

PURPOSE

The procedure is repeated to reinforce learning.

NARRATIVE

"Can you find another spot where Tate speaks?" Sherri asks.

Stacy finds it first. "'*I didn't know that was from a dog,*'" she reads.

"Underline those words," Sherri says, once again taking up the red pen and demonstrating on the overhead.

STEP NINE

When students find examples tagged with the pronoun *I*, review the reason for that pronoun.

PURPOSE
Reviewing the connection between the first-person pronouns and point of view strengthens student learning.

NARRATIVE

Sherri examines the words. "Notice it says *I*," she says. "Remember what Mark said. How do we know that *I* is Tate?"

Ashley has the answer first. "Because Tate is telling the story," she says.

"Right," Sherri responds. "It's from Tate's point of view."

STEP TEN

Once examination of the dialogue of the first speaker is complete on that page, search for the second character's dialogue. Use a different-colored pen to underline what that character says.

PURPOSE
To avoid confusion, Sherri chose to finish up the dialogue on one page before proceeding to the next page.

NARRATIVE

Students have covered all Tate's dialogue on that page so Sherri takes them back to find what Pap said. "Now, take out your blue crayon," she says. "Where is Pap speaking?"

Ashley reads, "*says Pap.*"

"What are the words that are coming out of his mouth?" Sherri asks. "Use the quotes to find them."

"'*If you're coming in, get on with it, Tate,*'" Ashley reads.

STEP ELEVEN

If necessary, prompt the student to look for quotes as signals to the beginning and end of the quotation. Continue to model the color-coded underlining.

PURPOSE
Questioning a student's decisions helps us to monitor his or her learning.

NARRATIVE

"Does Pap say anything else?" Sherri asks. Tim answers this time: "'*Ten is too young to work with saws and things.*'"

"Why did you stop after things?" Sherri asks. "Why didn't you continue?"

"Oh," Tim says and reads: "'*Besides, girls have plenty other jobs to do without messing with wood.*'"

"How did you know to read all that?" Sherri asks.

"I used the quotes to help find the end." Tim explains.

Following Sherri's model, students underline the words in blue.

STEP TWELVE

Write an example of a split quotation, such as: *"I have a dog," I said, "and his name is Bingo,"* and have students identify it.

PURPOSE

When we anticipate a possible problem, we provide an example in isolation that will activate students' memories.

NARRATIVE

"Who remembers what we call this kind of a quotation?" Sherri asks, changing the example on the board to: "I have a dog," I said, "and his name is Bingo."

Kevin's hand goes up. "Split," he says, glancing at the chart.

"Split quotation," Sherri says aloud, writing the words. "Exactly."

STEP THIRTEEN

Using the example as a model, have students locate a split quotation in the text handout.

PURPOSE

Students can use the model to find the example more easily.

NARRATIVE

"Let's see if we can find another one. Does Pap speak any more?" Sherri asks, prompting students to find the other split quotation.

Stacey reads this time: "'*Mam got herself tore up by a dog when she was a girl.*'"

"Why did you stop there?" Sherri asks. "Is that all Pap said?"

Stacey looks further. "'*You've seen that scar on her leg Tate,*'" she reads.

"How did you know that you weren't finished?" Sherri asks.

"I saw more quotes after *he said*," was her answer.

"And we call that a. . . ?" Sherri prompts, pointing to the board.

"Split quotation," Stacey reads.

STEP FOURTEEN

Ask for an explanation for the decision the student made. Underline the entire quotation in the color chosen for this character.

PURPOSE

Students should not only give the answer but explain *why*. We underline the quotation because, by studying the underlined words, students can recognize the format for a split quotation.

NARRATIVE

"Now, Stacey," Sherri continues, "how did you know to include *Tate*?"

"Because there weren't quotes until after Tate," she responds.

Sherri is pleased. One object of the lesson—to differentiate spoken words from the rest of the text in a split quotation—is beginning to take hold, at least with some students. Together, Sherri and the students underline Pap's words in blue.

STEP FIFTEEN

Find the remaining quotations. Make sure students have practice with split quotations and quotations longer than one sentence.

PURPOSE
Repeated practice reinforces learning.

NARRATIVE

Then, Sherri says, "We have to underline something else on this page. Who can find it?"

Tim finds the last quotation. "'*I didn't know that was from a dog,*'" he reads.

"Who said that, Tim?" Sherri asks.

"Tate," is his response.

"Underline that in red," Sherri directs students as she does the same on the transparency.

STEP SIXTEEN

Have students check to be sure all the dialogue has been identified.

PURPOSE
Students need to develop the habit of skimming work for possible omissions or oversights.

NARRATIVE

"Let's check now to be sure we found all the dialogue. Take your finger and place it at the middle of the page." Sherri demonstrates on the overhead. "Now let's trace down and look to the right and to the left to be sure we have not left out any quotations." She moves her finger slowly down the page, watching to see if students follow her. "Does anyone see any quote that we missed?" she asks.

Tim puts his hand up. "There's more that Pap said on page 10," he says. He reads: "'*You're letting the heat out.*'"

"You have sharp eyes, Tim," says Sherri. "That's the last part of another split quotation. Any more?" she asks, underlining the words Tim read in blue.

A chorus of "No, Mrs. Brecker," fills the room.

"Then we're finished for today," she says. "Tomorrow we'll look at all those words we didn't color in."

FOR YOUNGER STUDENTS

With first or second graders, teach this material over several lessons. Have each lesson focus on one element: the words or quotations, the punctuation, the name tags, and so on. The mentor text should, of course, be age-appropriate. Also, when underlining, it is not necessary to use a different color for each speaker.

Chapter 3: Writing Nonfiction

PORTRAIT OF A CLASSROOM WHERE NONFICTION MATTERS

Arriving at the William Winchester Elementary School in Westminster, Maryland, my step quickens. I tap lightly on Kathy Carhart's fifth grade classroom door.

"M-i-d-ge!" Kathy smiles and crosses the room to give me a bear hug.

"Hey, everybody, Dr. Madden's back! She's going to talk to us about writing feature articles and help us with our ideas."

I sit in the director's chair at the front of the room, watching and listening. Children sprawl everywhere, reading, writing, and talking about texts. After finishing an intensive historical fiction genre study, Kathy tells me that the class has decided to read and write about sports, but sports with a focus—inequities in the professional leagues.

"So, what do you think?" she asks, pulling over a chair. "The kids are really into this sports study and angry at the way women and blacks have been treated. They love your idea about writing articles and are anxious to see how to do it!"

"Great!" I smile at Tim and Ben, who wave. "If they're ready, let's begin." And I move to the overhead, lugging my notebook filled with transparencies of guidelines on writing feature articles, as well as professional and student examples.

"Hi, everyone!" I perch on an empty desk. "It's great to be back in one of my favorite classes talking about my favorite subject—writing!"

Ben makes a sour face and I laugh. "Come on, Ben. You're a good writer! And I know you're interested in sports. What I want to do today is walk you through the making of a feature article. Show you how one fifth grader develops his question, researches information, drafts, revises, and finally publishes. Alex— that's his name—even decides to submit his article to a children's magazine. And that's something you can all think about doing, too."

I begin by talking to the students about possible components in a feature article: strong voice, facts, opinion, and story, using a chart developed by Isoke Nia, a staff developer in New York City schools.

"Let's first look at Alex's argument, what we call his slant, in a feature article. Think about his title, 'Video Games Rock.' From this, what do you think his slant is?"

Tyler's hand shoots up. "It's definitely to show how good video games are." Several heads nod in agreement.

"Right, Tyler. Now listen to see if he writes a convincing argument." Putting the article on the overhead so that students can follow along, I read slowly. When finished, I wonder, "Hmmm . . . what do you think?"

Tim volunteers, "Well, he definitely uses some good facts . . . he gives his opinion, but he backs it up with facts."

"Okay, good, Tim. Let's look at his facts. That's the research part of a feature article. How do you think he gathers them?"

Maria offers, "Well, in social studies we learn that you can have primary and secondary sources."

Tyler adds, "Yeah, and here I think the primary is the info Alex gets from his survey. Secondary sources are, I guess, the quotes and facts he writes down from the Internet and video magazines."

"Excellent, Tyler! You guys already know a lot about this kind of writing. So, Alex uses opinion and facts in putting together his article. What about story or strong voice?"

"Well, there doesn't seem to be a story . . . and I'm not sure what strong voice is," says Tim.

"Okay. Anyone else confused here?" I look around the room, seeing a few hands rise and shoulders shrug. "Let me read the last part again: *I love video games and play them whenever I get a chance. I'll always be on the video games' side, and will love them no matter what. I hope you like them just as much as I do. Video games rock!*"

Johnny blurts out, "Oh, I get it! Strong voice means when the writer seems to be talking straight to you . . . like when Alex says *I hope you like them as much as I do.*"

"Right! So when you begin planning your articles and drafting, think of the four possible parts and try to include at least two. We see that Alex uses fact, opinion, and strong voice. But even more important, before you begin writing, you need to decide on the question that will become your slant. Take a few minutes now to talk to each other about possibilities; then we'll share."

The room buzzes with talk. Tyler and Johnny argue heatedly about whether umpires are impartial or not, and Ben and Brittany debate about discrimination against women in sports. Several others struggle to understand why whites make it difficult for blacks to get into sports.

I look at Kathy and grin. "They're definitely into this! I'm betting they'll write some strong feature articles!"

Kathy's is a classroom filled with animated talk, friendly argument, and endless questioning. In fact, her students always begin exploring topics with questions. "What about this topic really intrigues me?" "How can I find out more?" "What kind of writing do I want to do that best fits my topic?" They are not only learning that there are many kinds of nonfiction writing—such as biography, feature articles, and essays—but also that *good* nonfiction writing is more than a list of facts. As Tim says, "If I'm not excited about my topic, no matter how much research I do, it will be a flat piece. I simply won't care and it will come through in my writing." Yes, Tim, passion and curiosity drive writers of good nonfiction. Like you, they must first live the subject and form their own questions and opinions. First become an expert, then let the writing begin!

CHARACTERISTICS OF NONFICTION

In his book *On Writing Well*, William Zinsser uses the metaphor of carpentry to advise us about nonfiction: "Learn to hammer the nails, and if what you build is sturdy and serviceable, take satisfaction in its plain strength." A teaching unit on nonfiction will probably take longer than units on other genres because it involves not only teaching about writing, but gathering information about the topic from primary and secondary sources, sorting out the relevant from the irrelevant, and organizing the information into a "sturdy, serviceable" something that reflects "plain strength."

Once information is gathered, the writer must organize it into a logical whole. In the portrait that opens this chapter, we use a model drawn from a workshop given by Isoke Nia. She pointed out that in addition to the one expected feature that makes a piece nonfiction—facts—most nonfiction pieces have at least two of three other features: strong voice, story, and/or opinion. So, we need to show students how to sculpt their pieces, blending the facts they have uncovered with strong voice, story, and/or opinion. The end result will be pieces that entertain as well as inform.

Writing nonfiction is similar to writing fiction. In both cases, young writers need to plan before they begin to draft, envisioning the shape their writing will take. They need to start with an opening that grabs the reader, develop the idea, and finish the piece with an ending that will, to quote William Zinsser, "take your readers slightly by surprise but seem exactly right."

That said, the differences between the two genres are significant. Nonfiction—whether its purpose is to explain or to persuade—demands facts that support the premises introduced. In her workshop on non-narrative writing, Mary Chiarella of the Teachers College Reading/Writing Project, emphasized the importance of parallelism in introducing those ideas. While a piece of narrative usually moves sequentially through time, a piece of nonfiction develops logically, presenting the facts in an order that makes sense with respect to the thesis or theme of the piece.

Our purpose in writing plays an important role in the way we develop a nonfiction piece. A piece of expository writing, whose purpose is to explain, will differ from a persuasive piece, which will attempt to influence the reader's opinion. And while biography will inform us about the life of an individual, essays are best described as reflections, thoughts on a topic, or writing about ideas. As Stephanie Harvey puts it in *Nonfiction Matters*, "Essays make a point. The best ones make it in a powerful, literary way."

Students need strategies to help them develop written pieces that address these various purposes for, more than likely, sometime in their lives, they will be required to compose such texts. We need to teach them, for example, that in writing a persuasive text, their opinions count only when they are supported by reliable evidence. Too often young writers use the "others do" or "everybody says" argument, supplying information based on hearsay. They must also recognize that opinions that support the opposite point of view are acceptable, so long as they are also based on facts. We need to show students, too, that writing an essay will give them an opportunity to demonstrate the depth of their own knowledge on a topic.

EXAMPLES OF NONFICTION IN CHILDREN'S LITERATURE

Within the last decade, many nonfiction works written for younger children have emerged. Gail Gibbons, Joanna Cole, and Lois Ehlert are just a few of the many authors who have published well-written works on subjects from sea turtles to plants to space exploration. We provide books like these as references when we teach research in preparation for writing either expository or persuasive pieces. However, when introducing models of nonfiction, we prefer to use articles we find in children's magazines such as *National Geographic for Kids* or *Highlights for Children*. They are usually well organized and are about as long as we expect students' pieces to be. A list of such sources is included in Appendix A.

TECHNIQUES WRITERS OFTEN USE IN NONFICTION

In *Nonfiction Matters*, Stephanie Harvey writes, "The best nonfiction writing emerges from topics the writer knows, cares about, wonders about, and wants to pursue. It is in the pursuit of such self-selected topics that our students learn to apply the strategies we teach." The topics we ask students to consider

depend upon where we are in the unit of study. Mindful of Harvey's comment, we ask them in the beginning to select from a pool of topics about which they already know something. This allows us to skip over the need for research and move to a comparison between fiction and nonfiction. Once students have an understanding of the structure of a non-fiction piece, and understand how to plan one and draft one, we can move on to topics for which research is needed.

Within the latter category, we need to explain how to collect information. For primary sources, students need to understand how to observe and interview subjects. In seeking information from secondary sources, students must know how to use indexes and tables of contents. Knowing how to carry out searches on the Internet is also very helpful. Another important research tool they will need is a strategy for taking notes.

In this chapter, we give examples of some of the lessons we have used when teaching a unit on non-fiction writing. We encourage you to assess your students' work, decide on their needs, and use these lessons as models to design some of your own.

NONFICTION LESSON: Learning the Personal Interview

Taught by Midge Madden in Kathy Carhart's fifth grade class,
William Winchester Elementary School, Westminster, Maryland

William Zinsser, in *On Writing Well*, argues that the most interesting information is "locked inside people's heads," and *that's* the information a good nonfiction writer must unlock. So we teach students over time to master the personal interview. We discuss how to select a person to interview and why, always coming back to the idea of becoming knowledgeable about our topics. We brainstorm with students about selecting experts, model interview techniques, and teach students to write interview questions. This lesson focuses on teaching students the basic structure of an interview and how to write interview questions.

PREPARATION AND MATERIALS NEEDED:

- chart paper
- colored markers
- list of interview questions to use in a demonstration
- transparency of blank interview chart
- writer's notebooks
- pencils

STEP ONE

Introduce the lesson by telling students that many writers believe that the personal interview is one of the most effective sources of information. Ask students to suggest reasons why this might be true.

PURPOSE

By inviting students to suggest why interviews are important research tools, we learn what students already know about the interview process. More importantly, we show students that we value their knowledge.

NARRATIVE

"Remember when we talked about nonfiction writers and how they must first become experts about their topic? Today we're going to look at an important primary research source—the personal interview. Each of you will be conducting an interview for your feature article, so you'll need to know how to go about it. First, let's do some brainstorming. Why do you think an interview helps a piece of writing?" Students suggest reasons and I chart their ideas.

> ### STUDENT CHART ON WHY INTERVIEWING IS IMPORTANT IN GOOD NONFICTION WRITING
>
> - You learn about your topic "from the horse's mouth."
> - Interviewing makes your writing interesting, not just boring facts.
> - You can use direct quotes of an expert to support your argument.
> - Interviewing lets you get information that no book can tell you, like my grandfather was a survivor of the Holocaust and no book can tell his story as well as he can.
> - You feel like a newspaper reporter and can ask tough questions that you may or may not get an answer to.
> - Interviewing makes you really think about your topic and what you want to know. The more you know, too, the better your questions.

STEP TWO

Tell students that you and another adult are going to give a demonstration interview. Remind them that you want to learn as much as possible during the interview, since this may be your only opportunity to talk to the expert.

PURPOSE

Students learn interviewing strategies by watching a live interview, recording their observations, and discussing what they notice.

NARRATIVE

Students sit in a circle around the interviewee and me. "Listen carefully and write down your observations in your writer's notebooks," I say to the students. "I know you have watched interviews on TV, maybe the Oprah show or news reports. But today you're going to see a live interview. My friend, Gustav, from Paris, France, is visiting for a few days, and he has agreed to be interviewed. I am really interested in learning about Paris, since I'm traveling there this summer. As you listen to us, remember that although it may seem like a conversation, lots of preparation goes on before the actual interview. We'll talk more about that afterwards." I interview Gustav for about ten minutes, asking him a series of questions, some prepared ahead of time and some spontaneous, based on his responses.

PREPARED INTERVIEW QUESTIONS

- Why do people love to visit Paris?
- What are the most popular sights to see in Paris?
- What are some good small hotels where people also speak English?
- Can you go to the top of the Eiffel Tower? Notre Dame?
- Should I rent a car in Paris? I've heard that it's worse driving there than in New York City!
- How long have you lived in Paris?
- What are the places you visit again and again? Why?
- Are there things to see that most tourists miss? I want to do more than ordinary sightseeing things.
- Are there any special customs that I need to be aware of so that I don't offend anyone?

STEP THREE

Have students volunteer their observations about the interview. Chart their responses.

PURPOSE

Inviting students to study the interview makes them better researchers, as they notice details and ask questions.

NARRATIVE

"Okay, guys, what do you notice about this interview?"

"Gustav started by answering your questions," Tim observes, "then it seems like the things changed and Gustav was interviewing you."

"Yeah," adds Jared. "You are the one trying to find out about Paris, but Gustav asks you a lot of the questions, too."

"But did I learn about Paris?" I ask.

The students nod in agreement.

"I think you learned more than you thought you would," says Brittany. "I mean, your questions are all about tourist sights but Gustav gives you more, kind of like insider information—you know, he tells you about little hidden-away restaurants and uncrowded times to visit the Eiffel Tower."

Other students share their noticings and I chart them for future reference.

NOTICINGS ABOUT DR. MADDEN'S INTERVIEW

1. It seems like a conversation; both people are relaxed and not nervous.

2. Interviewer is not the only one who asks questions—Gustav seems interested in finding out what Dr. Madden really wants to do in Paris.

3. Dr. Madden learns things she didn't ask about—a bonus!

4. Gustav and Dr. Madden look at one another when they speak. Sometimes they nod their heads . . . maybe to show they agree with or understand each other.

5. Dr. Madden has a paper and notebook with questions, but she doesn't read from the notebook. I wonder if she memorizes the questions.

6. What does Dr. Madden write down? I hope we can read what she writes.

7. Interviewers take notes as the person being interviewed speaks.

8. Interviewers are fast writers!

STEP FOUR

Explain that good interviews happen *because* of good preparation. Discuss planning for an interview, focusing on the questions good interviewers ask. Explain that there are three useful kinds of questions: generic, personal, and follow-up (Harvey, 1998).

PURPOSE
Teaching students the preparation behind an interview helps them to plan their own interviews. Knowing the different kinds of interview questions is critical to good planning. Students learn to be flexible and see that good interviews cannot always be scripted.

NARRATIVE

"You noticed some important things about interviewing. One, especially, is that the interviewer must always try to create a relaxed atmosphere. Most people will be pleased that you see them as an expert and will be willing to share their knowledge. But a good interview involves more than simply chatting about a topic. We need much preparation *before* we interview. Good questions set the stage for a good interview. And there are three types of good questions: generic, personal, and follow-up.

STEP FIVE

Show students your prepared questions. Using a transparency showing the three kinds of interview questions, define each type of question, and record examples of each type from your interview. Invite students to join in wherever possible. Then, ask students if they remember any spontaneous or follow-up questions. Write these in column 3.

PURPOSE
By thinking aloud and charting types of questions from the demonstration interview, we help students understand how to construct their own interview questions.

NARRATIVE

"Watch me as I categorize the questions that I asked Gustav," I say. "Join in whenever you can. We will include any follow-up questions that you have recorded in your notebooks, too."

I begin charting my questions in the appropriate column, thinking aloud as I write. "Hmm . . . my first question, 'Why do people love to visit Paris?' is, I think, a generic one. It's not really personal, about Gustav. But my next question, 'As a Parisian, where do you go over and over again? Why?' . . . Hmm . . . that's definitely a personal one."

Students begin to contribute their thinking and together we fill in the chart.

THREE TYPES OF INTERVIEW QUESTIONS		
Generic questions	**Personal questions**	**Follow-up questions**
Why do people love to visit Paris?	How long have you lived in Paris?	You say that you only know Paris because you've lived there all your life. It seems like a beautiful city in which to live. But are there any parts of the city that I should avoid, or can I walk everywhere?
What are the most popular sights to see in Paris?	What are the places you visit again and again? Why?	
What are some good small hotels where people also speak English?	Are there things to see that most tourists miss? I want to do more than the ordinary sight-seeing things.	
Can you go to the top of the Eiffel Tower? Notre Dame?		You mentioned that some Parisians don't like American tourists and that you once had a bad experience with a group from New Jersey. Can you tell me more about that?
Should I rent a car in Paris? I've heard that it's worse driving there than in New York City!	Are there any special customs that I need to be aware of so that I don't offend anyone?	

STEP SIX

Ask students to think about who might be an expert on their topic, give them a few minutes to talk with a partner, and invite volunteers to share.

PURPOSE
Focus shifts from teacher-led to student-led. In order to apply new learning, students must be given the opportunity to try out their thinking.

NARRATIVE
"Where might you find someone to interview about your topic? Who might be your expert? I want you to share your thinking with a partner for a few minutes. Then we'll brainstorm some of your ideas together."

STEP SEVEN

Have students share some of their ideas about possible experts and begin writing interview questions. You might want them to work in pairs. Post the completed question chart for easy reference. As students work, roam around the room, talking to them and providing help. Have students try out their questions on you, pretending that you are their expert.

PURPOSE

Students need time to think more about their topics in light of who can provide information on it. Writing sample interview questions with an expert in mind helps them to delve deeper into their topics and to plan their interviews.

NARRATIVE

"Let's share some of our ideas for experts." I listen to volunteers who explain who their experts might be and where to find them. Then I say, "Now, I want you to try writing your own interview questions. Keep your expert in mind as you draft questions. Remember, you most likely will not ask all of your questions. Also remember that follow-up questions can't be planned because they follow from an answer to a previous question. I'll be coming around to hear your ideas. Some of you may want to try out your questions on me, and that's great. I'll be happy to play your expert!"

After experimenting with writing interview questions, invite students to share some of their questions. Guided by you, students begin to see the types of questions that yield useful information about topics.

TYPES OF INTERVIEW QUESTIONS

Generic: General questions about the topic of the interview. For example, a question about the climate in Paris would be a generic one.

Personal: Personal questions seek specific information about the ideas, opinions, or experiences of the person being interviewed. For example, *What is your favorite restaurant in Paris?*

Follow-up: Questions based on a question or comment during the interview. Such a question seeks further information. For example, the interviewer might follow up the personal question above with *Why is it your favorite restaurant?*

FOR YOUNGER CHILDREN

Students in first and second grade, under the guidance of the teacher, can prepare questions for an interview. The teacher might conduct the interview, using the student-generated questions. After the interview, students and teacher can chart the information they learned. Identifying the types of questions can be omitted in lessons for younger children.

THREE TYPES OF INTERVIEW QUESTIONS		
Generic	Personal	Follow-up

NONFICTION LESSON:
3-2-1 Note-Taking Strategy

Taught by Midge Madden in Kathy Carhart's fifth grade class,
William Winchester Elementary School, Westminster, Maryland

In learning to write good nonfiction, we first teach students to follow their interests and passions in selecting a topic. But once a topic is chosen, students need to become experts. They must learn ways to collect and synthesize information—to act as researchers tapping primary and secondary sources. While the previous lesson focuses on primary research by teaching about interviewing, this lesson helps young writers to glean information from secondary sources. Pulling out and paraphrasing important information presents difficulties for many students. Using a simple heuristic like 3-2-1 helps them to do this. Students learn to select big ideas, synthesize, and ask questions—researching strategies that lead them to more questions, deeper digging, and, finally, becoming experts.

PREPARATION AND MATERIALS NEEDED:

- transparency of an excerpt from an information piece (See the example I wrote, "The Mysterious Monarchs' Journey," p. 88)
- transparencies of 3-2-1 blank template and teacher 3-2-1 model
- student copies of 3-2-1 blank template and text used

STEP ONE

Tell students that nonfiction writers are researchers who use primary and secondary sources to find important information about their topic.

PURPOSE
Students learn that research is critical to good nonfiction writing.

NARRATIVE

I begin, "You know, when you're truly interested in something, you're willing to search to find out more. My daughter, Lisa, is expecting her first baby in two months, and she reads all she can find about pregnancy and having a healthy baby. She asks doctors and nurses about delivery and the anesthesia risks. She asks other women what their labor was like. Everywhere she goes she looks for more information to add to what she already knows. And this is just what good nonfiction writers do. They pick something that puzzles them or that they just have to find out more about . . . and then they begin searching."

STEP TWO

Tell students that they are going to learn a way to take notes in order to get information from secondary sources, such as magazines, books, and the Internet.

PURPOSE

Most students have a difficult time taking notes. As writers/researchers, they need to understand how to extract and synthesize new information.

NARRATIVE

"Today we're going to learn a strategy called 3-2-1 that writers use to collect information about their topics. I'm going to show you how it works, using a text about monarch butterflies, *my* topic. Yesterday, I visited a kindergarten class that was studying monarchs. One little girl grabbed my hand and pulled me towards the window sill to see their caterpillars. 'They're going to turn into butterflies,' she announced. 'And do you know, whole groups of people track these butterflies' trip to a place in Mexico?' I didn't know that! So now I am looking for more information. This excerpt is something I wrote after reading all about the monarchs' migration."

THE MYSTERIOUS MONARCHS' JOURNEY
Midge Madden

They come from the East Coast and the Midwest every winter . . . thousands of black-and-orange winged beauties flying south. And the destination is the same small spot of forest in Mexico. For the monarch followers who wait in Mexico, the sight is astounding. A drab patch of brown forest becomes transformed into a shimmering world of color, a sea of brilliant oranges reminiscent of the vivid hues of a New England fall.

For thousands of years, the monarch butterflies have been congregating at this same place in Mexico. Scientists have long puzzled over this phenomenon, suggesting many possibilities for an answer. Some speculate that butterflies have an internal homing device; others believe that light and sunshine play an integral part in guiding the monarchs' journey. And as scientists study further, they are learning that memory alone does not explain the amazing ability of these butterflies to migrate.

Now a new wrinkle has appeared. Still trying to determine the why's of the monarchs' journey, scientists have discovered that the small patch of forest in Mexico is slowly disappearing. And the wintering butterflies need thick clusters of trees for shelter from wind and rain. Logging in Mexico has not only resulted in deforestation, but threatens to end the monarchs' migration.

STEP THREE

Read aloud the excerpt from teacher text displayed on the overhead. Think aloud about important ideas and personal responses to the text.

PURPOSE

Students need to see and hear how proficient readers think about new information found in texts and how they decide which information to record.

NARRATIVE

I read aloud the excerpt from the transparency while students silently follow along. Then I say, "Hmmm. There's lots of new information here, but I don't want to write all of it down. I'm interested in monarch butterflies, but my big question is about how they travel such long distances to the same exact spot. So, if that's my focus, I definitely want to remember that butterflies have been making this same journey for maybe thousands of years. And maybe, the location. Oh, and also the idea that memory isn't what guides these butterflies on their journey."

STEP FOUR

Place the transparency of the blank 3-2-1 template on the overhead. Introduce the template as a framework to use in taking notes from texts. Explain that writers record three things they want to remember about their topic in column 1. Model by writing three facts from the text you are using.

PURPOSE

Students learn how to pull out pertinent facts about their topics by observing the teacher's model and think aloud.

NARRATIVE

I tell students we will focus on filling in the first column of the template. I say, "In the first column, we write three things that we want to remember about our topic. We have to always keep our big question in mind; for example, mine is, 'How do monarchs travel to such a far destination?'" I record the three ideas that I have voiced aloud, using my own words as much as possible.

BLANK 3-2-1 CHART

3 Facts	2 Surprises	1 Question

STEP FIVE

Explain that in column 2 of the chart, writers record two things that surprise them about their topic. Write down two things in the second column.

PURPOSE

Students learn how to synthesize and discover surprising facts by observing the teacher's model and think aloud.

NARRATIVE

Referring to the second column of the transparency, I think aloud about ideas that surprised me. "Hmm . . . I never even thought about migrations stopping. How do scientists know that the forests are disappearing? And if monarchs don't use memory, how do they find their way? I guess I'll record the ideas that the forest is disappearing and monarchs don't rely on memory." I write these two ideas in column 2.

STEP SIX

Pointing to column 3 on the template, tell students that here writers record a question they still have. Write the question in the third column.

PURPOSE

Students need to see how to complete a heuristic or framework before they can try it out on their own. They also need to understand how asking questions drives further inquiry.

NARRATIVE

I display the text about monarchs on the overhead and reread it aloud. Then I display the model template, rereading what I have written in columns 1 and 2. Finally, I ask, "What question do I still have?" I think, then write, "What will happen to monarchs if the migrations come to an end?" Reading aloud, I reflect, "The more questions I write, the more questions I have."

TEACHER 3-2-1 CHART

3 Facts	2 Surprises	1 Question
Monarch butterflies have made this journey for thousands of years.	Migrations will stop because the forest is disappearing.	What will happen to monarch butterflies if their migrations end?
They migrate to a location in Mexico.	Monarchs don't use memory to find their way.	
Memory isn't what guides these butterflies on their journey.		

STEP SEVEN

Have students try out the 3-2-1 strategy with their own nonfiction text (book, magazine article, newspaper article, Internet print-outs). Each student should read one page or one section, then fill in a blank template.

PURPOSE

Teachers can determine whether students understand a new strategy when they can use it to record information for their own research topic.

NARRATIVE

I pass out blank 3-2-1 templates to each student and direct them to try to fill in the template on their own, using a preselected text on their topic. I move around the room, helping students as needed. For closure, students pair-share their 3-2-1 charts.

STUDENT 3-2-1 CHART

3 Facts	2 Surprises	1 Question
The biggest and most commplete T.*rex* skeleton in the world was found in South Dakota.	Sue was as big as a double decker bus, weighing over 14,000 pounds.	How did Sue get put together?
The T.*rex* Sue is named after scientist Susan Hendrickson who found it.	One footstep would reach 12-14 feet.	
Sue's bones were in the best condition anyone has ever seen.		

Alex , Fourth Grade
Notes from *A Dinasaur Named Sue* by Pat Rief

BECOMING EXPERTS

Students can use the 3-2-1 strategy to gather information from various secondary sources. Each question they ask in column 3 provides a focus for further research, driving the inquiry. When ready to draft their piece of writing, students use multiple 3-2-1 charts as their research notes. They review information gathered and questions answered. Tapping and reflecting on all of this new knowledge, students become experts on their topic. Then they begin to write.

NONFICTION LESSON: Studying the Structure of an Information Piece

Taught by Jane Sullivan in David Jackson's fifth grade class,
Upper Township Elementary School, Upper Township, New Jersey

We usually move more slowly in a unit on nonfiction than we do in a unit on memoir or fiction. The reason for this is that there are so many structures to learn. For example, a simple information piece, a reflective essay, and a persuasive piece are just a few of the forms nonfiction takes. Each one is built differently. To study the structure of an information piece, we use a graphic organizer entitled "Information Piece" (based on Isoke Nia's work) because it helps students visualize the components more easily.

PREPARATION AND MATERIALS NEEDED:

- a sample of a short information piece that illustrates the structure, such as Mary Kay Carson's article "Balloon with a View" (*Super Science*, May 1993, pp. 14–17)
- a chart listing clues to characteristics of good writing
- transparency and photocopies of the graphic organizer titled "Information Piece." On the transparency, the individual boxes should be covered with sticky notes that will be removed during the lesson.
- individual copies of the article you choose

STEP ONE

Read aloud with students the article you have chosen, making sure that students comprehend the major ideas.

PURPOSE
Students need to be familiar with the entire article before analyzing the structure.

NARRATIVE

"Let's take a look at this article," I say. "Find page fourteen in your copies. Anyone want to take a guess as to what it's about?"

Miles's hand shoots up. "Weather balloons?"

"Well let's see." I read the first paragraph. "Was Miles right?" I ask.

Haley answers my question. "Partly, it's about weather balloons but it talks about Mars so it must be a balloon that they sent to Mars."

"This doesn't sound like a fiction story to me. What do you think?"

Joe skims the article and raises his hand. "It's nonfiction," he says.

I agree. "How did you decide that?" I ask.

"It looks like it's giving information about these balloons," he says, pointing to the pictures.

"Okay, let's read and see if Joe is right." I read the rest of the article, pausing to discuss the information as we move through it. Now we are ready to analyze the structure.

STEP TWO

Prompt students to analyze the article for examples of one of the four features we find in a well-written information piece: strong voice, opinion, story, facts. In this step, I began with "voice." The order in which each feature is discussed is not critical. What is critical is that students understand the difference between facts, a feature *always* present in nonfiction, and the three other features which are *sometimes* present.

PURPOSE
Asking students to analyze text, with guidance from the teacher, enables them to take charge of their learning. Identifying the four features will help them decide how to structure the information pieces they will write.

NARRATIVE

"Let's take a look again at the first two sentences in this article. Not what it says but how the author says it," I say. "What do you notice?"

SammiKate is the first to respond. "She's talking to us."

"And how did she do that?" I ask.

"She uses 'you' like I'm right there with her," SammiKate continues.

"So, it's like she's having a conversation with us," I say. "What do we call that in our writing?"

Students are familiar with the concept "strong voice," so it isn't difficult for Miles to come up with that answer.

STEP THREE

Call attention to the chart that lists characteristics of good writing. Review the techniques writers use for strong voice. Find other examples of such techniques in the article you are using.

PURPOSE
Several examples will clarify the concept of strong voice.

NARRATIVE

I continue the inquiry. "What are the ways we put strong voice into our writing?"

Steve recalls what we have said about strong voice in past lessons. He answers. "With questions or when you use *I, we* and *you*."

I call attention to the chart hanging at the side of the room. "And that's what our chart says, isn't it?" I say. "Any other examples of strong voice in this article?"

Students find several.

CHARACTERISTICS OF GOOD WRITING SHOW, DON'T TELL

Use:
- strong voice: questions, *I, we, you*
- dialogue
- inside/outside story: thoughts, feelings/ dialogue, actions

---

STEP FOUR

Place the transparency "Information Piece" on the overhead. Lead students to understand that strong voice is not always found in nonfiction writing.

PURPOSE
Recognizing those features that are sometimes present in nonfiction writing will assist students when they plan their own writing.

NARRATIVE

"Here's a chart that will help us remember the features of an information piece. Do we always find strong voice in this kind of writing?"

Lexis shakes her head. "Not in my math book," she says. "It doesn't sound like anyone's talking to me. It just tells me what to do."

I remove the sticky note from the "Strong Voice" box. "See—I've written strong voice here on the right-hand side of our chart," I say. "Lexis is right. We'd like to find strong voice in an information piece, but it isn't always there. So, I list it on this side along with other features that are sometimes there."

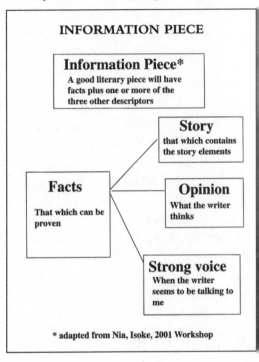

STEP FIVE

Direct students' attention to facts in the article. Remove the sticky note from the "facts" box on the information piece chart.

PURPOSE
Students need to know that facts are the primary feature of an information piece and are always present in nonfiction writing.

NARRATIVE

"Let's see what else we can find," I say, reading the next sentence: *In the 1970s, scientists sent robotic probes. The probes landed on Mars—but they were stuck in one spot.* I ask, "What is the author doing now?"

Dennis scratches his head. "She's telling us stuff?" he offers.

"Okay," I say. "And what kind of 'stuff' is she telling us, Dennis?" He tries again. "True stuff?"

"Yes, it is true. We can look it up and see that it actually happened, stuff we can prove. So what can we call that kind of stuff?"

Adam tries this time. "Facts?"

"Facts is a good answer," I say. "And in this kind of writing, writing that gives us information, do we always find facts?" I ask.

"Sure," Dennis says. "That's what information is. Facts."

Once again, I call students' attention to the chart. "Since we *always* find facts in an information piece, it should be over here, on the left. Let's see if that's what's in this box. I remove the sticky note to reveal "Facts" and the definition.

STEP SIX

Discuss the possibility of story as part of an information piece. Since we do not find story as a feature in the article we are analyzing, I refer to another article with which students are familiar.

PURPOSE

Comparing this article with another one with which students are familiar helps them to realize that story is another feature sometimes present in nonfiction. They can use this information when writing their own information piece.

NARRATIVE

"Remember that article we read the other day about wild horses? Do you remember what you noticed about that piece, Adam?" I ask.

I want students to recall that sometimes authors "tuck" little stories into nonfiction. Adam commented on this just a few days ago. He remembered. "Yeah, I said it sounded like a story."

I nod. "Is there a story in this article?" I ask, pointing to the balloon article we are working on.

A chorus of voices responds: "No!"

"So, we only find story sometimes. That's another box we can fill in on the right side of our chart." I remove the sticky note from the "Story" box. "We can put a personal experience into our writing in nonfiction, if we choose," I say. "A little story."

STEP SEVEN

Direct students' attention to examples of opinion in the article.

PURPOSE

Students should also realize that information articles sometimes include opinion.

NARRATIVE

"Let's read the next section again," I say. "We've already said that question is an example of using strong voice." I read the next sentence aloud: *Scientists are planning to send one. But it will only be able to drive about 1/2 km (1/3 mile) a day.* "What would you call that?" I ask.

"A fact?" says SammiKate.

What about the next sentence? I read: *You can easily walk that far in 7 minutes.*

"My grandmother wouldn't walk that far in seven minutes," says Miles. "So, that isn't a fact. It's opinion."

"It may be what you think but not necessarily what everyone else thinks," I say, expanding the concept. "Does opinion have to be there?"

Students shake their heads. I remove the sticky note from the remaining box, saying, "Opinion: what the writer thinks."

STEP EIGHT

Review the four features of an information piece.

PURPOSE

Reviewing the entire model helps students conceptualize the pattern.

NARRATIVE

"Let's review: An information piece will always have . . ."

Students read: "Facts," as I point to that part of our chart.

"I put that by itself. Why?"

After a pause, Britney suggests, "Because it can be proved?"

"That is correct about a fact but it isn't why I put it all by itself, over here," I respond.

Jake raises his hand. "Because it's always there."

"Good thinking, Jake," I say. "In an information piece you will always find . . ."

"Facts!" Everyone calls out to my prompt.

"On this side, I listed the three characteristics that an information piece will have . . . ?"

Students pick up the rhythm and, once again, reply together: "Sometimes."

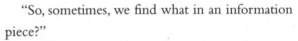

"So, sometimes, we find what in an information piece?"

"Story, opinion, strong voice," is once again the choral response.

FOR YOUNGER CHILDREN

For second and third graders, select text that is age-level appropriate. Examine various texts for examples of facts and opinions. Children should discover that facts are always present in nonfiction. Opinion is sometimes present. In subsequent lessons, guide students in writing their own information pieces.

NONFICTION LESSON:
Planning a Persuasive Essay

Jane Sullivan, taught in David Jackson's fifth grade class,
Upper Township Elementary School, Upper Township, New Jersey

Students disagree. It is a fact of life. We can help them channel that natural behavior into persuasive writing by teaching them to argue with purpose and logic. We do this by showing them how to design a plan for a piece of writing that will persuade readers to agree with them. That is what this lesson is all about.

In the classroom where this lesson took place, we had already studied an article that argued for keeping the natural habitat of monarch butterflies intact. In this lesson, we refer to that article to teach students how to design a persuasive essay of their own.

PREPARATION AND MATERIALS NEEDED:
- chart listing arguments about a specific topic (See the List of Reasons Why We Should Save the Forests Where Monarch Butterflies Winter, on page 98, based on the article "The Mysterious Monarchs' Journey" from the 3–2–1 Note-Taking lesson.)
- transparency and photocopies of a blank graphic organizer for writing a persuasive essay
- transparency of blank teacher's graphic organizer
- teacher's example of a completed essay
- copies of blank chart

STEP ONE

Review how we distinguish between fact and opinion.

PURPOSE
We need to reinforce what may be a recently introduced concept for some of the students.

NARRATIVE
"Okay," I say, "think about the discussions we had when we studied information pieces. We listed some details that we called facts and some that we called opinions. Who can tell me how we tell the difference between fact and opinion?"

"If you can prove it, it's a fact," says SammiKate. "When you have an opinion about something, it's how you think about it. But not everybody thinks the same way. Like I think *The Indian in the Cupboard* is a good book, but Haley doesn't really like it."

"That's a pretty good explanation, SammiKate," I respond. "You can't argue with a fact. You can argue with someone else's opinion, though."

STEP TWO

Introduce the purpose of today's lesson.

PURPOSE
We establish the purpose to give students a mindset, a way of thinking about where we are headed.

NARRATIVE

"Today, I want to talk about writing to persuade our readers. It is writing based on our opinion. We call it a persuasive essay." I hand Adam copies of the labeled chart to pass out while I put a copy of it on the overhead. "This is the plan I use when I write a persuasive essay," I explain.

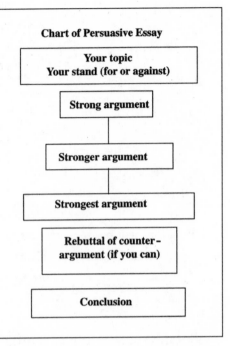

Chart of Persuasive Essay

Your topic
Your stand (for or against)

Strong argument

Stronger argument

Strongest argument

Rebuttal of counter-argument (if you can)

Conclusion

STEP THREE

Analyze a persuasive piece students have read to introduce the concept of writing to persuade. Identify the author's topic and stand, or viewpoint.

PURPOSE
Students need to learn that in a persuasive essay the writer identifies the topic—and his or her position on that topic—in the first paragraph.

NARRATIVE

"Now, we have said it wasn't surprising to find opinion in a nonfiction piece, one that just gives us information. Think about the article we read on monarch butterflies. Do you think that author just wanted to give us information?" I put up the chart we made when studying that article.

Haley raises her hand. "In that last paragraph, I think she was trying to persuade us to save the forests where the butterflies live."

I return to the chart on the overhead. "After reading the article on monarch butterflies, we decided two things: First, her topic." I point to the phrase *Your topic* in the chart. "Which was?"

"Monarch butterflies?" offers Steven.

Lexis's hand goes up. "Not just that! It talks about saving the forests where they migrate to."

I nod. "Can you see, Steven, how the author took just a little piece of information about monarch butterflies—where they live—and talked about that?"

Steven nods.

I continue. "What do you think the author's stand is, her point of view?"

Steven, checking the chart, once again responds. "She's for it."

LIST OF REASONS WHY WE SHOULD SAVE THE FORESTS WHERE MONARCH BUTTERFLIES WINTER

For: We shouldn't let logging take away the forests:
- When you cut down trees, the butterflies will have no protection.
- Without the trees, rain will wash the soil away.
- Without forests, water will be muddy. People won't have water to drink or to wash in.

Against: Allow loggers to cut down the trees:
- The people are poor. They need to sell the wood for fuel.

Rebuttal: Cutting down trees won't work
- When the forests are gone, there won't be any wood left to sell.

STEP FOUR

Identify the reasons the author gives in support of that stand.

PURPOSE
Students need to learn that it is necessary to provide factual support for the stand a writer takes on a particular topic.

NARRATIVE

"What reasons or arguments did she give us that make her think that way?" I ask, pointing to those boxes on the chart.

Miles answered this time. "Butterflies need the trees to protect them against the wind and rain."

"And they're deforesting Mexico," SammiKate added.

"Which will make . . . ?" I prompt.

". . . the soil wash away." SammiKate completes my sentence.

STEP FIVE

Identify the rebuttal used to refute a counterargument.

PURPOSE
Students need to learn the role a counterargument plays in a persuasive essay and how to refute such an argument.

NARRATIVE

"But what about the people?" I ask. "Who remembers what we said about them?"

"They need the money they get from selling the wood," says Joe.

"So, we thought of an argument against saving the butterflies' home, what we call a counterargument. Yes?" I point to that phrase on the chart.

"Yeah," says Joe. Only then we said if they cut down the trees, pretty soon they'd all be gone. Then, the people wouldn't have any trees to make money, anyway."

"In other words, the author gave us a look at one side of the story, and we figured out another side and also why that wasn't a good reason. We *refuted* the argument the other side might use." On the board, I write: "A rebuttal refutes a possible counterargument." Then I ask, "But what if we hadn't thought of a good reason, if we couldn't refute it?"

Miles speaks first. "Keep quiet?"

"Right," I say. "Don't give the other side any ideas."

STEP SIX

Model the plan you would use to write a persuasive essay. Using the labeled chart, show students the topic and stand you would take.

PURPOSE

Students learn when we show rather than tell them what to do.

NARRATIVE

"If I'm going to write an essay, I need to plan, too. I think cutting down trees will be my topic and my stand or point of view will be that we need to do it wisely." I put a transparency of a blank teacher's chart on the overhead and write those words in the top box.

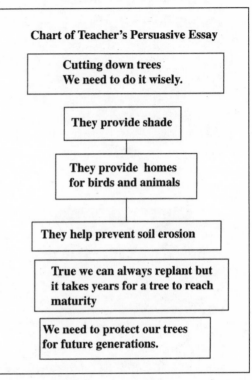

Chart of Teacher's Persuasive Essay

> **Cutting down trees**
> **We need to do it wisely.**

> **They provide shade**

> **They provide homes for birds and animals**

> **They help prevent soil erosion**

> **True we can always replant but it takes years for a tree to reach maturity**

> **We need to protect our trees for future generations.**

STEP SEVEN

Show students three reasons that support your stand. Have students arrange them in order of strength.

PURPOSE

Providing at least three reasons to support your stand on the topic makes for a strong argument. Arranging them so that the strongest reason is given last also increases the power of your argument.

NARRATIVE

"Let's think about the next three boxes. I'll write my reasons there. First, let me show you the reasons I have for cutting down trees wisely." I write the three reasons on the chalkboard in random order: *They help prevent soil erosion. They provide homes for birds and animals. They provide shade.* Look at the three boxes on your handout. How do I need to arrange these reasons?"

Sean reads the words in each of the three boxes: strong, stronger, strongest.

"So, I need to decide which one is the strongest."

"Which one do you think is my strongest reason, Britney?" I ask.

Britney thinks a bit, then reads: *They help prevent soil erosion.*

"So, that reason would go last," I say, numbering it #3.

Students identify the other two reasons by strength. I write the reasons in the appropriate boxes on the transparency of my chart.

STEP EIGHT

Review the objective of a counter-argument.

PURPOSE

Students may need to be reminded that we sometimes must argue against an objection.

NARRATIVE

Returning to the chart that defines each section of the essay, I say, "Next, I have to decide if I have anything to put in this box." I point to the rebuttal box. "But, if I put in a reason that the other side might use, what must I do here?"

Miles raises his hand. "You need to refute it," he says, glancing at the chalkboard.

"Very good, Miles. And I liked the way you used that word *refute*. What does that mean?" I ask.

Miles thinks, then responds, "Shoot it down," he says.

The students laugh. I smile. "You could say that, as long as you don't mean that literally!"

STEP NINE

Provide an example of a counterargument and its rebuttal.

PURPOSE

Students need to understand that, in the logical order, the counterargument would be introduced last.

NARRATIVE

I continue. "Now, I need to think first of an argument the other side might use against me. Well, let's see. They may argue that you can always replant the trees. Now, how could I refute that? Any ideas?" Lexis waves her hand in the air. "The other day," she says, "you told us how you cut down that big tree in your yard and how you found out that it was 110 years old."

I nod. "And, so . . ."

Lexis continues, "Well, a tree takes a long time to grow. So if you take down an old tree and plant a baby one in its place, you might be dead before it's big."

"A good way to refute that argument," I say. "Does everyone agree?"

Students nod. "So I can put in a counterargument in this box and what my rebuttal will be." I write these words in the rebuttal box: *True, we can always replant—but it takes years for a tree to reach maturity.*

STEP TEN

Show how the conclusion sums up your opinion.

PURPOSE
A conclusion that sums up an opinion ends on a strong note.

NARRATIVE

"One box to go," I say, pointing to the conclusion box on the graphic organizer. "What shall I put here? What do you think?"

"In the monarch article, she kind of warns us," says Haley. "The monarchs won't migrate."

I agree. "So I could end my essay the same way, couldn't I? I might say: We need to protect our trees for future generations." I write that in the last box.

STEP ELEVEN

Review the steps you took in modeling the plan.

PURPOSE
A review such as this one helps to pull the parts into a logical "whole."

NARRATIVE

"So, let's see what we have here. What did I decide first?" I ask.

Steven calls out. "Your topic and your stand."

Then what did I have to think about?"

Miles answers this time. "Your reasons why you think that," he says.

Adam chimes in. "And you have to put them in order—strong, stronger, strongest."

"And . . ." I prompt.

"Then, you think of your counterargument," offers Britney, stumbling over the word *counterargument*.

"And . . ." my prompting continues.

"And how you can refute it," Miles says, now confident of the word *refute*.

"Which brings me to here," I say, pointing to the conclusion.

"You need to think up a real strong ending," says SammiKate. "One that says it all—like *We need to think about a future without trees*."

"Good job, SammiKate," I say. "That says it all."

STEP TWELVE

Explain that you will take each idea from the plan and write a paragraph based on it, containing facts and examples.

PURPOSE
Students need to see the diagram as a blueprint from which to write their persuasive piece.

NARRATIVE

"Later," I say, "I am going to take this plan and use it to write my essay. I'll take the idea in each box, develop it and add details so my reader will understand exactly what I mean. Each of the ideas will become a separate paragraph."

STEP THIRTEEN

Distribute blank copies of the diagram to students and brainstorm on a topic they can all write on.

PURPOSE

After observing the teacher plan a persuasive essay, students need to try out the strategy themselves in # order to understand better the function of a graphic organizer.

NARRATIVE

"Now, I'd like you to fill in a diagram like mine," I say. "Let's suppose we're writing a letter to the editor to share our opinion about something. What could you write about?"

Hands go up all around the classroom. "A better park." "Trash in the streets." "Supporting our troops."

Satisfied that most have topics, I move on. "Okay, you have to come up with three reasons why your idea is a good one or a bad one. Fill in your chart. You may work with your partners. I'll come around and help."

"What about the counterargument?" Adam asks.

"If you can come up with one," I say, "fill in that box, too. But you may not have a counterargument. Then, leave it blank."

Before my words are finished, the room is filled with the buzz of conversation. Students are ready to plan.

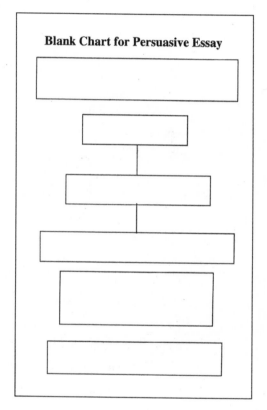

Blank Chart for Persuasive Essay

FROM PLANNING TO WRITING

Once I am satisfied with the students' ability to plan a persuasive essay, I model how to use the diagram as a basis for essay writing. On my own, I write an essay and then share it with students. We compare my completed chart with the essay so that students can see how I fleshed out each idea with details. Then I'll ask them to write their pieces as a letter to the editor of the local newspaper, following the charts they have prepared.

TEACHER'S PERSUASIVE ESSAY BASED ON COMPLETED CHART
Jane Sullivan

It was a cool Sunday morning in October when we cut down the tree. It was a 110-year-old stately oak, but it was in the way. Such a frivolous reason: it was in the way.

When trees disappear, their valuable contributions disappear as well. Trees, for example, store water and, later, release it into the atmosphere, providing water for plants and animals who depend on it. Destroying this water storage unit creates a drier climate. In addition, the roots of the trees we destroy no longer hold down the soil. Wind and rain erodes the topsoil, washing it away into lakes and rivers. Those trees that were "in the way" could have prevented that.

We once thought the giant redwood forests of California were in the way. From 1905 to 1929, about 500 million board-feet of redwoods per year were cut down. That number rose to a billion between 1947 and 1958. The majority of these ancient trees were used for lumber. Finally, the government put a stop to the cutting. The small fraction of these huge trees that remain are now protected. They are no longer looked upon as "in the way."

When we protect our forests, we protect the plants and animals that live there as well. New Jersey has about one million acres of undeveloped land called the Pine Barrens. Pigmy pines, smaller than ten feet in height, grow there. It is the largest pigmy-pine forest in the country. Rare and interesting plants grow in the New Jersey Pine Barrens. The bog asphodel, for example, does not grow anywhere else in the world. Orchids such as the beautiful white fringed orchid grow there, too. Thirty-nine species of animals considered threatened with extinction, such as the barred owl and the northern pine snake, live in the Pine Barrens. This forest has been designated a biosphere reserve by the United Nations and a "Last Great Place" by the Nature Conservatory. Fortunately, New Jersey residents do not consider the pigmy pines of the Pine Barrens to be "in the way."

The greatest danger we face in cutting down our forests is climate change—what scientists call global warming. Living trees store carbon dioxide, a major "greenhouse" gas. When we cut down trees, this gas is released into the atmosphere. If the greenhouse effect raises the earth's temperature, forests may not be able to survive. Once considered "in the way," they will disappear. Future generations will need to survive without the benefits such forests provide.

There are so many reasons why we need to conserve our forests. Next time we decide to nail a board to an oak tree or bulldoze a pine tree that is "in the way," we should stop and think about the consequences. Maybe before it's too late, we'll learn ways to coexist with these friendly giants.

STUDENT'S PERSUASIVE ESSAY

Dear Editor:

I think our American soldiers are brave. They left their families to go fight the war. They are constantly under fire. They are fighting terrorists who could use chemical weapons.

It must be hard to leave your family. You might die and then your family would be left alone. Or you might miss your new baby. If you're away, you can't play or talk to your children. That is one reason why the soldiers are brave.

There is a second reason why the soldiers are brave. They are constantly under fire. They are brave, even though Tanks are firing Artillery shells at them.

Terrorists can possibly use chemical weapons. The soldiers wear gas masks and chemical suits even when the temperatures are over 100°. They have to try to destroy chemical weapons. Sometimes Something could go wrong and they might get blown up.

Brave soldiers are my models. Brave soldiers are not just my model, they are my heroes.

Sincerely,
Jayson

FOR YOUNGER CHILDREN

For students in second and third grade, use a single paragraph format: the lead sentence provides the topic and the stand of the writer. Three subsequent sentences provide arguments in support of the stand. The closing sentence reiterates the opening sentence. The following is an example:

I think we should preserve our trees. Trees provide shade. They act as homes for birds. Their roots hold the soil so rain can't wash it away. Trees are our friends and we should always protect them.

NONFICTION LESSON:
Writing a Literary Essay

Taught by Jane Sullivan in David Jackson's fifth grade class,
Upper Township Elementary School, Upper Township, New Jersey

As we reflect on the parts that stand out for us once we've finished a good book, we embark on a "journey of thought" that helps us make sense of what we have read. Recording those reflections that search for meaning in the author's message is what writing a literary essay is all about. In this lesson, we show how we teach children to write such an essay.

PREPARATION AND MATERIALS NEEDED:

- copies of a short story to read aloud (We used "Eleven" from *Woman from Hollering Creek* by Sandra Cisneros.)
- photocopies and transparency of the blank web template
- blank transparencies
- student notebooks/writing journals

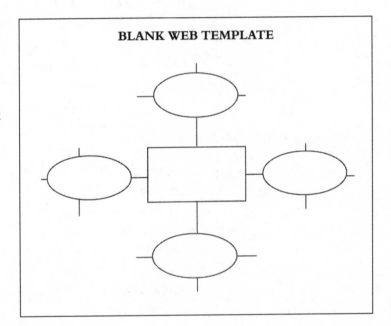

BLANK WEB TEMPLATE

STEP ONE

Read aloud the short story to students. As you read, pause periodically and think aloud about the reflections you have on the ideas you read.

PURPOSE
Students can use your reflection as the foundation for the essay they will write collectively.

NARRATIVE

"Read along with me as I read this short story aloud. I am going to stop and think about each section as I read it." I read the first section where Rachel, the narrator, reflects on her age. "While I was reading, I was thinking," I say. "I sometimes feel like I'm five when I see a scary movie. I understand how Rachel feels." I continue reading, stopping and sharing my thoughts about Rachel's plight. I invite students to take over the think-aloud, encouraging them to express their thoughts on the thoughtless girls, the unsympathetic teacher, and Rachel, who wishes she was 102, so that a painful experience would be erased from her memory.

Teaching the Elements of Powerful Writing

STEP TWO

Explain to students that the purpose of an essay is to write about our ideas—our opinions—on a particular topic. In writing a literary essay, we share our reflections on a book or short story we've read.

PURPOSE

Students need to understand that to write a literary essay, they must recall their reflections on an important issue in the selection and present them in a logical order.

NARRATIVE

Laying the book aside, I glance at students. "Powerful, isn't it? Made me want to hug Rachel and tell her I'm sorry. How many of you felt that way?" Hands go up around the room.

"I really did not like that Sylvia," says Emily. "She's mean."

"And what about that teacher?" Adam adds. "She wasn't nice, either."

I smile at their reaction. "What I want to do today," I announce, "is gather up all the thoughts we had as we read Rachel's story, organize them, and write a piece we call a literary essay."

STEP THREE

Discuss students' thoughts about what happened in the story in # order to help them plan the organization of the essay.

PURPOSE

Brainstorming together gives students the opportunity to learn from their peers.

NARRATIVE

"Adam and Emily have already shared some of their thoughts. What other ideas did you have as we read this piece?" I ask.

Hands go up around the room. I nod to Lexis.

"I thought of the set of dolls I have. Like the one that Rachel has."

"Say more about that," I prompt.

Haley continues. "It's true. I have years inside me, like all of my dolls fit inside the biggest one.

"And . . ." I say.

"And sometimes I don't feel ten even though I am."

Miles joins the conversation. "I remember on my birthday, I didn't feel any different."

"So," I say, picking up my black pen, "you think one of the big ideas in this story is how you're . . ." I wait for a response.

Jason answers. "You're still all you did in the past."

"What other big ideas did you have?" I ask. "Think of the conversations and the actions of Rachel and her classmates. Think about the reactions, too. How Rachel or Mrs. Price or Sylvia or Phyllis reacted to what was happening."

I replace the transparency of the web template with a blank transparency. One by one, students give me their ideas, and I list these on the transparency.

LIST OF BIG IDEAS

- You're still all you did in the past.
- You remember the bad things.
- You're eleven but you don't feel like it.
- Teachers always seem to think they have to be right.
- Silence gives consent—guilt makes us honest.
- You are other years as well as this one.
- You don't always feel the age you are.

Of the ideas listed, have students select what they consider to be the biggest or most important of the ideas—the theme.

PURPOSE

Showing students how to identify the theme or "biggest big idea" of a story will help students arrange their reflections logically around that theme.

NARRATIVE

"Let's look at what we have listed here. See if we can find one idea that would include all the others—our 'biggest big idea,'" I say.

We read the list together. Mike raises his hand. "I think it's the last one," he says, "You don't always feel the age you are."

"Say more about that, Mike," I prompt.

"Well, all the others kind of fit inside that. Like, if you think teachers are always right and you get mad at your teacher 'cause she's wrong, you're like a little kid."

I want to hear more of this logic. "And . . . "

Mike thinks a little, then continues, "Well, 'cause we know teachers aren't perfect. No one is."

"Everybody agree?" I ask.

Ashley speaks up. "And you do remember all the bad things that happened to you and then you feel like you're that old when you do."

I am satisfied that we have chosen our theme. I put up a transparency with the web outline I have prepared. "We can call the 'biggest big idea' the theme. I'm going to write the theme in the center box," I explain. I write: "People are more than one age—like rings on a tree." I ask students to draw a box in their notebooks and I do the same.

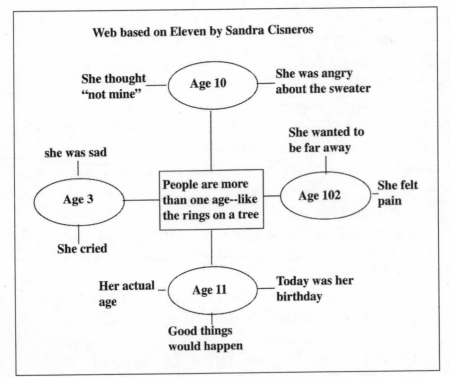

Web based on *Eleven* by Sandra Cisneros

STEP FIVE

Complete the web by adding details from the story that support the theme.

PURPOSE

Students need to be able to demonstrate that their choice of theme is a logical one, supported by details the author has included.

NARRATIVE

I ask students to look again at their copies of "Eleven." "You have chosen as the theme that people are more than one age. Now you need to explain why you think that. What details can you find in the story that support that as the biggest big idea?" One by one, they give the ages Rachel mentions in the story to prove that she believes people are more than just one age: 10, 102, 11, 3. I write the ages in the circles that surround the center box.

STEP SIX

Have students find examples that explain the circled entries.

PURPOSE

Identifying minor details that explain the supporting details will help students flesh out the essay they will write.

NARRATIVE

"Now, let's take each one of these ages and see if we can find details about them in our story. Why do you say that sometimes people are the age of three?"

Joe responds. "That's when you're sad or you cry."

I write those words on the lines extending from the circled three. "And ten?"

Jason has this one. "She was angry about the sweater. That's a little stupid."

"And she cries, 'not mine,'" adds Emily.

We continue. For 102, the students agree that Rachel would be far away from embarrassment and pain, that she would be able to tell Mrs. Price she was wrong. For eleven, they listed that today was her birthday, her actual age and that good things would happen at home.

From the ideas on the web, begin writing an essay as a class.

PURPOSE
Writing as a group allows students to take part in composing but does not require that they take complete responsibility for the task.

NARRATIVE

"Now, we've done all the planning. We're ready to write a literary essay. Remember, it's going to sound like a journey. We're going to describe the ideas and thoughts we had as we read. We retell a part of the story only to explain our thoughts. But, before we begin that part, what do we need to write?"

Mark calls out, "Strong lead."

I smile. My teaching has taken hold. "Absolutely. Any ideas about a strong lead we can use, Mark?"

"We could use the center box," he suggests. "People are really all different ages instead of just one age."

"And we could say that in 'Eleven,' Rachel compares her age with rings on the inside of the trunk of a tree," says SammiKate.

"And then we could go to each one of those circles and talk about the age in there, starting with three," Joe suggests.

As students contribute their ideas, I write them on the transparency. We work back and forth, reflecting on each of the ages, expanding on the idea, until the essay is complete.

GROUP ESSAY: "ELEVEN"
(FROM *WOMAN OF HOLLERING CREEK*, SANDRA CISNEROS)

People are really all different ages instead of just one age. In "Eleven," Rachel compares her age with rings on the inside of the trunk of a tree.

When you cry, Rachel said, you feel like you are three. Rachel cried. She made animal noises. She spit. She fell into a tantrum like she was three.

When you say something stupid, you are ten. Rachel stuttered out, "that's not, I do not, you are not . . . Not mine," when Mrs. Price stuck the sweater on her desk. That was a stupid thing to say. Rachel was acting like she was ten.

She felt ten, too, when she whined about the sweater. It is just a sweater. I did not do anything to her. And yet, she still whined about it. In the course of a lifetime, what does it matter?

Rachel wished she were 102. If she were 102, she would be older and wiser than Mrs. Price. Therefore, she would have known what to say. Then, the pain would all go away. Rachel wished that she could be "far away . . . like a runaway balloon." Being 102 would make that happen.

When we read this story, I felt like I was looking into a literary mirror. I wanted to hurt the teacher. I was acting like I was four. Sandra Cisneros made me feel that way. "Eleven" reminds me sometimes of all my ages. I am always going to be those ages.

STEP EIGHT

Review the steps followed in developing the essay. As students recall each of the steps you followed, write them on a chart and display it where students can see it.

PURPOSE

Reviewing the steps prepares students for writing a literary essay on their own.

NARRATIVE

"Now, we've finished our draft. So, let's review the steps we followed," I say. "Who remembers what we did first?"

Adam answers first. "We read the story."

I write these words on chart paper, then prompt, "To . . . ?"

Adam finishes, "to understand it?"

I finish the sentence with *for comprehension* and look for a volunteer to give me the next step. Soon we have all the steps listed.

"Now, I want you to think about the book you just finished. Do you think you can do the same thing with that story? Write a literary essay about it?"

Students nod their heads.

"Okay, take out your notebooks and the book you were reading. What will you do first?"

Emily knows. "Look for big ideas that made you think a lot?"

"And then . . . ?"

Jason provides this answer, glancing at our chart. "Pick the biggest big idea," he says.

"I think you're ready," I say. "You write, and I'll come around and help anyone who has a question."

Students locate their writing tools, then settle down to collect their thoughts, eager to write their own essays.

STEPS IN WRITING A LITERARY ESSAY

- We read the story and got a good understanding of it. And we did a think-aloud.
- We looked for the big ideas.
- We listed the big ideas.
- We picked the biggest big idea.
- We made the web.
- The center was the big idea.
- Around it, we put details.
- We found examples that helped show the details better and wrote them next to each detail.
- We wrote the essay.
- We used the biggest big idea in the lead.
- We used the details and the examples for each paragraph.
- We wrapped up our essay in the ending paragraph.
- We revised.
- We edited.

EMILY'S ESSAY: *THE WANDERER* **BY SHARON CREECH**

One Friday afternoon in July, I watched the waves break over the shore. I watched the white foam flow over the shore and run back into the water. I was glad not to be inside the wave and to be near death. In *The Wanderer*, that is what happened to Sophie as a little girl. She was under the water swirling and twirling looking for the surface.

Sophie did get out of the wave but she didn't remember that it happened. Later, she had dreams about a giant black wave coming toward her and crashing into her. Every time she woke up from her dream, she felt as if she was floating in the water. Then that feeling went away.

I have also had dreams that try to tell me certain messages such as what could happen in my near future. Well, the dream Sophie had about the giant black wave may be trying to send her a message. A wave in reality is white; the wave in the dream was black. That is a mystery.

Another giant mystery was about the real parents of Sophie and their disappearance. Sophie tells stories about her life through little kid stories. The stories are actually about her own life experiences. She tells them about her parents and herself.

In the story, *The Wanderer*, Sophie has to figure out the many mysteries of her life. She tries to figure out her mysteries just as we are trying to figure them out for ourselves.

JACOB'S ESSAY: *THE WANDERER* **BY SHARON CREECH**

Jacob   June 3

Literary Essay

In Sharon Creech's, The Wanderer, a girl named Sophie, has many dreams of a big wave. This wave is a big black towering wave.

This dream scares her very much. She has this dream very frequently and is so afraid of it. She always wakes up just when the wave is going to crash on her. That huge wave may be connected to her parent's death.

The little kid stories, that Sophie tells, are a mystery. But, the little kid might be Sophie. She's maybe trying to hide herself as a small child. In the little kid story on p. 98 she tells how she was looking for her parents, but they were somewhere else. Also on p.209 she sys how she was hearing a voice in her head screaming, "Mommy, Daddy!" This happened when the real big wave hit.

In all of my dreams, bad dreams, I wake up, it goes away, and I never have that same dream again. But it is different with Sophie. Sophie keeps having the big wave dream. It keeps coming back to haunt her.

FOR YOUNGER CHILDREN

For students in second and third grade, you may want to adapt this lesson for use following a read-aloud of a book. Have children select a particular character or event. Ask them to reflect on reasons why they liked (or did not like) that character or event. Under your guidance, have them create a paragraph, using their reasons. The first sentence should tell the reader which character will be discussed and the point of view of the book's author. The next several sentences should explain why the writer chose that point of view. The final sentence can sum up or repeat the writer's point of view.

Epilogue
The Beginning

I sit in Kathy Carhart's room in William Winchester Elementary School, poring over final drafts of historical fiction pieces written by her fifth graders. I am awed by the power of their work. Their writing pulls the reader in with tension-built plots, and vividly captures a moment in history. Paul offers me his story and I read an excerpt:

> *"Bayonets ready," the general ordered. "Charge!"*
>
> *Joey, I, and the rest of the brigade began to run towards the enemy. All I could hear were guns firing, people yelling, and the thumps of men falling. We struck the confederates like a colony of ants feeding on a fallen cracker. I swung at every moving thing I saw.*
>
> *Then it hit me. I felt something sink deep into my chest. Pain filled my body. I began to feel dizzy, trying to keep my balance. I dropped my gun and fell. Men were running over my arms and legs, although I could not feel it as much as the pain in my chest. I looked around at the men. I could not see Joey. I began to gasp for breath. Everything went black.*

"So, what do you think, Dr. M.?" Paul asks with a frown.

I smile and reply, "I think you have written a gripping scene, Paul. I can feel the battle as I read and I want to go on."

"Well, thanks, Dr. M." Paul sighs his relief. "I worked on this for a long while and I think I have it right now. I know now that writers revise again and again!"

Learn it. Try it. Write it. Question it. The students in Kathy Carhart's class learn first what good historical fiction sounds like. They learn writing techniques such as dialogue, character development, creating settings, and building tension in a story. Then they try putting it all together in a piece of writing. And they question: "What can we do to make it better?"

Learn it. Try it. Write it. Question it. So we leave you with these words. We know that writing, writing about writing, and teaching about writing can never be finished. So we title the epilogue "A Beginning." And we invite you to journey with us as we continue to explore the possibilities of writing in genres.

In *The Fifth Season*, Robert C.S. Downs writes beautifully about the awakening of a sixty-year-old son. As his father battles the cancer ravaging his body and his mother "drifts ever deeper into the midnight of her own brain," Teddy Neel understands his purpose in a moment of brilliant clarity. He says: *What comes to me is that this is not the most important time of their lives, but of mine. I was sent here to learn, even to be tested. This is my journey, too.* At sixty, Teddy is just beginning to understand aging, its inevitable approach and consequences. While life has come full circle for his parents, he takes comfort, realizing that this is an important time in his life as well. Understanding much, he also accepts that there is still much to know. And he embraces the challenges of this new journey.

Becoming a writer and a teacher of writers is a never-ending journey, marked by moments of cleared seeing. Like Teddy, new understandings await as we explore new ideas. In *One Writer's Beginnings*, Eudora Welty writes: *As we discover, we remember, remembering, we discover; and most intensely do we experience this when our separate journeys converge.* She suggests that becoming a writer requires linking the looking back and the looking forward to the here and now in our lives. In Kathy Carhart's classroom, students such as Paul continually look back on what they have learned: about history, about fiction, about writing, and about themselves. In so doing, they write better, crafting powerful pieces.

We hope that this book will inspire you to continue to write, and if you aren't writing yet, to begin. Start a writer's notebook. Look at your world through inquisitive and eager eyes. Ask questions. Seek answers. Then ask the same of your students. You have read our argument that writers and teachers of writers must have a strong knowledge base before they can write. Learn the genres and the crafting techniques that characterize these genres. Use our lessons to become more skilled at writing in various genres and in teaching students to write in these genres. Collect mentor texts—good examples of fiction, memoir, and nonfiction. Investigate to learn what makes each genre work. Write to deepen your understanding. Then use *your* writing as mentor texts and watch as your classroom writing community emerges.

Finally, this book is not simply about the process and products of teaching writing. We provide no ready-made answers. Rather, it is about a journey that we took as writers and teachers of writers, practicing and revising our theory of teaching. We hope the book speaks to you about the importance of taking an inquiry stance on your own practice as writing teachers.

We continue to teach and we continue to learn. Each time we meet a new group of students, our hearts quicken with anticipation and eagerness—anticipation of what this new group of writers will teach us, and eagerness to begin again. We know that each class determines its own possibilities. And we wonder what new writing discoveries await us. Come join us on our journey.

> *"Words are my gun and my spear,"*
> *sings the aboriginal storyteller.*
> *Teaching writing, we seek so to*
> *arm our students.*
> *Weaving ideas into tangible wholes,*
> *We write as our students write . . .*
> *Endless possibilities, catching thoughts,*
> *Writing visions of a world*
> *Known and yet unknown.*

Appendix A
Some Books and Magazines to Use as Model Texts for Writing

MEMOIR

Bridges, Ruby. (1999). *Through My Eyes*. New York: Scholastic.

Burleigh, Robert. (2003). *Into the Woods.* New York: Atheneum Books.

Byars, Betsy. (1991). *The Moon and I*. New York: Simon & Schuster.

Cisneros, Sandra. (1991). *The House on Mango Street*. New York: Vintage.

Dahl, Roald. (1984). *Boy*. New York: Puffin Books.

Greenfield, Eloise. (1993). *Childtimes*. New York: HarperCollins.

— (1988). *Grandpa's Face*. New York: Philomel Books.

Gray, Libba Moore. (1995). *My Mama Had a Dancing Heart*. New York: Orchard Books.

Grimes, Nikki. (2002). *Talkin' About Bessie*. New York: Orchard Books.

Hesse, Karen. (1999). *Come On, Rain*. New York: Scholastic.

Howard, Elizabeth Fitzgerald. (1991). *Aunt Flossie's Hats (and Crab Cakes Later)*. New York: Clarion Books.

Jiang, Ji Li. (1997). *Red Scarf Girl*. New York: HarperCollins.

Little, Jean. (1987). *Little by Little: A Writer's Education*. New York: Viking.

— (1990). *Hey World, Here I Am*. New York: Harper Trophy.

Lowry, Lois. (1998). *Looking Back*. Avenel, NJ: Random House.

Naylor, Phyllis Reynolds. (1987). *How I Came to Be a Writer*. New York: Aladdin.

Nixon, Jean Lowery. (2002). *The Making of a Writer*. New York: Delacorte Press.

Polacco, Patricia. (1994). *My Rotten Redheaded Older Brother*. New York: Simon & Schuster.

— (1992). *Chicken Sunday.* New York: The Putnam & Grosset Group.

— (1994). *Firetalking*. New York: Penguin Books.

Rylant, Cynthia. (1984). *Waiting to Waltz.* New York: Simon & Schuster.

— (1982). *When I Was Young in the Mountains*. New York: Dutton.

Sender, Ruth Minsky. (1986). *The Cage*. New York: Simon & Schuster.

Smucker, Anna Egan. (1989). *No Star Nights*. New York: Alfred A. Knopf.

Snicket, Lemony. (2002). *Lemony Snicket: The Unauthorized Autobiography*. New York: Harper Collins.

Spinelli, Jerry. (1998). *Knots in My Yo-yo String*. New York: Alfred A. Knopf.

Strickland, Michael. (2001). *Haircuts at Sleepy Sam's*. Honesdale, PA: Boyds Mills.

Tarpley, Natasha Anastasia. (2002). *Bippity Bop Barbershop*. Boston: Little, Brown & Co.

Yolen, Jane. (1992). *Letting Swift River Go*. Boston: Little, Brown & Co.

FICTION WITH A STRONG SENSE OF STORY

Brinkloe, Julie. (1985). *Fireflies*. New York: Simon & Schuster.

Cooney, Barbara. (1990). *Hattie and the Wild Waves*. New York: Puffin.

Crews, Donald. (1992). *Shortcut*. New York: Greenwillow.

Dahl, Roald. (1964). *Charlie and the Chocolate Factory*. New York: Puffin.

Fox, Mem. (1984). *Wilfrid Gordon McDonald Partridge*. New York: Kane/Miller.

Havill, Juanita. (1986). *Jamaica's Find*. Boston: Houghton Mifflin.

Kellogg, Steven. (1986). *Best Friends*. New York: Penguin Group.

L'Engle, Madeleine. (1962). *A Wrinkle in Time*. New York: Farrar, Straus and Giroux.

Lowry, Lois. (2000). *Gathering Blue*. New York: Random House.

MacLachlan, Patricia. (1980). *Through Grandpa's Eyes*. New York: HarperCollins.

— (1991). *Journey*. New York: Bantam, Doubleday, Dell.

Paterson, Katherine. (1987). *Bridge to Terabithia*. New York: Harper Trophy.

Paulsen, Gary. (1987). *Hatchet*. New York: Puffin Books.

Rylant, Cynthia. (1985). *Every Living Thing*. New York: Aladdin Paperback.

Sachar, Louis. (1998). *Holes*. New York: Farrar, Straus and Giroux.

Yashima, Taro. (1955). *Crow Boy*. New York: Penguin Group.

Woodson, Jacqueline. (2001). *The Other Side*. New York: Putnam.

NONFICTION

Information

Brown, Margaret Wise. (1949). *The Important Book*. New York: Harper & Row Publishers.

Cole, Joanna. (1987). *The Magic School Bus Inside the Earth*. New York: Scholastic.

Ehlert, Lois. (1987). *Growing Vegetable Soup*. New York: Harcourt Brace.

Gibbons, Gail. (1992). *Stargazers*. New York: Scholastic.

Pallotta, Jerry. (1991). *The Furry Alphabet Book*. Watertown, MA: Charlesbridge Publishing.

Ryan, Pam Muñoz. (1996). *The Flag I Love*. Watertown, MA: Charlesbridge Publishing.

Simon, Seymour. (1995). *Sharks*. New York: HarperCollins.

Essay

Baylor, Byrd. (1977). *The Way to Start a Day*. New York: Aladdin Paperbacks.

Carlstrom, Nancy White. (1997). *Raven and River*. Boston: Little Brown & Co.

Farris, Christine King. (2003). *My Brother Martin*. New York: Simon & Schuster.

Henkes, Kevin. (1981). *All Alone*. New York: Greenwillow.

Libby, Barbara. (1993). *Old Cat*. Avenel, NJ: Random House.

Rylant, Cynthia. (1998). *Scarecrow*. New York: Harcourt Brace.

— (1996). *The Whale*. New York: Scholastic.

— (1991). *Appalachia*. New York: Harcourt Brace.

Schuett, Stacey. (1995). *Somewhere in the World Right Now*. New York: Alfred A. Knopf.

Siebert, Diane. (1991). *Sierra*. New York: HarperCollins.

Stewart, Sarah. (1997). *The Gardener*. New York: Farrar, Straus and Giroux.

Zolotow, Charlotte. (1992). *The Seashore Book*. New York: HarperCollins.

Persuasive

Baylor, Byrd. (1986). *I'm in Charge of Celebrations*. New York: Aladdin Paperbacks.

Rylant, Cynthia. (1991). *Night in the Country*. New York: Aladdin Library.

Waber, Bernard. (2002). *Courage*. Boston: Houghton Mifflin.

CHILDREN'S MAGAZINES

Boys' Quest. Bluffton, OH

Cricket. Carus Publishing Company, Cricket Group, Peru, IL

Guideposts for Kids. Guideposts, Carmel, NY

Highlights for Children. Honesdale, PA

Hopscotch for Girls. Bluffton, OH

Kids Discover. New York, NY

Ladybug. Carus Publishing Company, Cricket Group, Peru, IL

National Geographic World for Kids. National Geographic Society, Des Moines, IA

Ranger Rick. National Wildlife Federation, Vienna, VA

Spider. Carus Publishing Company, Cricket Group, Peru, IL

Super Science Blue. Scholastic Inc., Jefferson City, MO

Weekly Reader. Weekly Reader Corporation, Stamford, CT

Appendix B
Some Books With Ideas for Teaching Writing

Angelillo, Janet. (2002). *A Fresh Approach to Teaching Punctuation*. New York: Scholastic.

Atwell, Nancie. (1998). *In the Middle, New Ed*. Portsmouth, NH: Heinemann.

— (2002). *Lessons That Change Writers*. Portsmouth, NH: Heinemann.

Bomer, Randy. (1995). *Time for Meaning*. Portsmouth, NH: Heinemann.

Calkins, Lucy. (1994). *The Art of Teaching Writing, 2nd Ed*. Portsmouth, NH: Heinemann.

Downs, Robert C.S. (2000). *The Fifth Season*. Washington, DC: Counterpoint Press.

Elbow, Peter. (1998). *Writing with Power*. New York: Oxford University Press.

Fletcher, Ralph. (1993). *What a Writer Needs*. Portsmouth, NH: Heinemann.

— (1993). *Breathing In, Breathing Out*. Portsmouth, NH: Heinemann.

Fletcher, Ralph & J. Portalupi. (1998). *Craft Lessons*. York, ME: Stenhouse Publishers.

— (2001). *Nonfiction Craft Lessons*. Portland, ME: Stenhouse Publishers.

Fox, Mem. (1991). *Radical Reflections*. New York: Harcourt Brace.

Gardner, John. (1983). *On Becoming a Novelist*. New York: WW Norton & Co.

Goldberg, Natalie. (1986). *Writing Down the Bones*. Boston: Shambala.

— (2000). *Thunder and Lightning*. NY: Bantam Books

Graves, Donald. (1994). *A Fresh Look at Writing*. Portsmouth, NH: Heinemann.

Harvey, Stephanie. (1998). *Nonfiction Matters*. York, ME: Stenhouse Publishers.

Hayes, Christopher. (1996). *English at Hand*. Marlton, NJ: Townsend Press.

Heard, Georgia. (2002). *The Revision Toolbox*. NH: Heinemann.

Hindley, Joanne. (1996). *In the Company of Children*. York, ME: Stenhouse Publishers.

Holdaway, Don. (1979). *The Foundations of Literacy*. New York: Ashton Scholastic.

Kelton, Nancy Davidoff. (1997). *Writing from Personal Experience*. Cincinnati, OH: Reader's Digest Books.

King, Stephen. (2000). *On Writing*. New York: Scribner.

— (1999). *The Girl Who Loved Tom Gordon*. New York: Scribner.

Noble, William. (1991) *Show, Don't Tell*. Middlebury, Vermont: Paul S. Eriksson.

Ray, Katie Wood. (2002). *What We Know by Heart*. Portsmouth, NH: Heinemann

— (2001). *The Writing Workshop*. Urbana, IL: NCTE

— (1999). *Wondrous Words*. Urbana, IL: NCTE.

Welty, Eudora. (1983). *One Writer's Beginnings*. Cambridge, MA: Harvard University Press.

Zinsser, William. (1998). *On Writing Well*. New York: HarperCollins.

— (1988). *Writing to Learn*. New York: Harper & Row.

Appendix C
Complete Texts of Student Writing Samples

Here are three complete student pieces—memoir, fiction, and nonfiction writing—that speak to the possibilities of children who write. These are not meant to be used as model texts for mini-lessons. We hope, rather, that they might offer you ideas for constructing lessons in your writing classroom. Read, listen to these young voices, be swayed in your thinking, but critique as well. What do these students do well? What more needs to be taught? And how best can we teach such burgeoning writers?

Through Alex's Eyes

Mmmm. Mangoes. Huh? Oh hi. Can you guess who I am? I'm smart, I'm a good friend. I'm the Boogie Man!! No, just kidding. I'm really Alex Aguayo. My mom's African American and my father is Mexican. I am nine and a half years old. I have a little brother named Tony who is now seven. I wear glasses and I love bubble gum. My favorite flavor is fruit tornado. I also love dinosaurs, gem stones, Pokémon and animals. I lived with my mother and father for the first four years of my life. Now I live with my Mommom and Pops.

Thinking back to my early years, I remember my preschool graduation. I had no shoes on since I had stepped in dog poop! I was running on the playground and I tripped, bumped my head, and fell in "doo doo"! The teachers didn't want me to track dog poop in the school so I wore only socks. I remember Aften and Qortney. They were my two best friends. I also remember wearing a white dress with a purple skirt on my head. I was the one who liked to build the most out of all the kids in the class.

Once on a cold Christmas morning, I remember the first present I opened was a star charm with two crystals and a bow. When my mom gave it to me, she said, "You are my star and always will be." Our Christmas tree was brimming with cat ornaments. When we were opening the ornaments, I noticed how pretty they were. Some had spirally glitter. Some had a bell inside a bell inside a bell inside a bell inside a bell. There were lots of cat ornaments. Some cats were flying fish kites, some had mouse parachutes, some were stuffed and soft, some were wooden and solid, and some were made of glass. One cat ornament was a picture frame with my photograph in it.

Once on a cold Christmas morning, I remember our whole family came over for dinner. We had juicy steak, chewy shrimp, steaming turkey, marinated salad, and mashed potatoes. Turkey was my favorite! It was moist and juicy. We had lots of yummy things. That was one Christmas that I'll never forget.

Once on a cold Christmas morning, I remember our family was together for the last time. I remember my Nana and my Aunt Naomi being smoking "buds" out on the porch. Aunt Naomi had an Internet boyfriend named Duke whom I've never seen. Aunt Naomi also loved to take me to the river and feed the ducks. Nana had a dog named Sunshine. He would always have little squeaky toys that I would always squeeze and he would wonder what the noise was. I remember some of the toys were things like a squeaky frog and dinosaur. I miss Sunshine. I miss Aunt Naomi and Nana too. Aunt Naomi with her wigs that I loved (as well as her bears) and Nana with her dog, Sunshine. Now they're both stars in the sky.

Alex O is my best friend. He is square, has green-ish brown eyes and chubby cheeks. Alex O is real sensitive about wearing a bathing suit. He is very self-conscious about his weight and can have his feelings hurt very easily. We both have the same name, but what I think made us friends most of all is that when I first entered Tatem, I was crying. He asked me, "Do you want to sit next to me?" That made me feel much better. We've been friends ever since.

Alex O is good at being a friend too. For example, if he can play in a game and I cannot, he won't want to play. One time when we joined a club, Jack was chasing and tagging us. When he tagged me, I said, "I take three hits." They kicked me out of the group because they thought I was changing the rules when they had never even said any rules. The leader, whose name I forget, said, "You cannot be part of this group." So, Alex O. said, "Then I am not going to be part of this group either."

We both like the same things like the Legend of Zelda series. He is interested in frogs, dinosaurs, reptiles, and Pokémon. He loves T-rexes and that's why he likes Jurassic Park movies. When we played the Pokémon Stadium 2 Game, he defeated a lot of trainers. His favorite Pokémon are Logia, Ho oh, Mewto, Pichu, and Clefairy. I cannot name the rest because he changes favorites every week and I can't say a hundred and fifty-two names!

I remember going to get my first Ocicat, Bogie. "Oh goody goody gum drops!" I was thinking to myself inside. I can't wait to get to Bogie's old house. His new house is going to be my house! I was as excited as a squirrel winning a whole jackpot of pistachios!

When we got to the breeder's house, the first thing I see are two big, beautiful, gorgeous cats with stripes and spots and a dog lying on his belly. I start scratching his belly. While I am scratching him, one of the breeders goes upstairs to get Bogie who is sleeping. He is so darling. The breeder puts him in my arms. He says, "Go to your daddy, Bogie." We brought a new carrying case and so I put him in. From the way he is crying, I can tell he is thinking, "Where on earth am I?" I sing to him a lullaby that I heard from the "Prince of Egypt." Before you know it, he is practically asleep. This is one moment that both of us will never forget.

Well, that just about wraps it up for my memoir written at age nine. I wonder what else on the road of life awaits me. It could be good; it could be bad. Who knows . . .

Alex Aguayo, Grade 4
Tatem School, Haddonfield, New Jersey

The Uncivil War

Introduction

A book that tells how many men became soldiers and how boys became men and farms became battlefields. No real plot in itself, but welcomes you to imagine the horror of battle. Using words that shortly describe hate truly tell the story. It's really your imagination that tells how this soldier feels and lives through two short battles.

I

November 11, 1861
Clayton, Louisiana

Dear Diary,

I called my Ma as I walked through the maples. Their bark was rough rugged and barren. The leaves turned a reddish hue. As I came through the clearing I saw my pigs. They had been rosy pink even though last year's winter wasted a lot of them. They quickly scuttled off in fear of going to the slaughterhouse. Suddenly the peaceful night sky was shattered by the sound of battle. "What's happening?" I wondered. It became hazy. I had nearly stepped foot onto the battlefield and I became part of the swirling red hurricane of hate. The pigs were madly being slaughtered by the Yankees' bullets and nothing could escape this battle. Our cows fell like soldiers to water. I . . . felt saddened.

Rotating I saw something shocking, my house burning like hell was eating it. And I visioned the loss, my ma and pa and sis gone. Upon this thought I was driven mad, my head boiling. Yankees had raided my home. What I deemed impossible had become real. We heard the North wanted us to become one of them and give up our president. Since we had calmly answered no (We did not feel it was really a true friendship. They demanded our president to be handed to them; we were angered.). They needed to use force. Us rebels wanted political freedom and fought to defend ourselves. Though we did not have many soldiers, all of them were veterans, each one special. We thought we could take them. But now I know otherwise. I was red hot mad thinking about this. I ran blindly as long as my swollen legs could bear my weight. I struggled to push myself forward. I did and I got into the shattered town of Columbia.

November 19, 1861
Columbia, Louisiana

Dear Diary,

Columbia seemed a worse sight than my own home. It was dreary. Soldiers were not really soldiers; they were like me: lost their homes to the Yankees and ran. They marched solemnly into the mist. Surely I was not one of them but as I looked in a puddle I saw a grave face with the same fear as those soldiers. I rushed quickly to join their slow line of grief. The soldiers were ragged in terms of clothes; some had no shoes. I was the same. We marched till we heard the sound of Yankees. The General told us to aim at their legs. I did not know what to do until I picked up the rifle of a dead soldier. His lifeless eyes gazed at me almost to warn me not to take the burden. I took the rifle and fired making the night sky glow a luminescent yellow. The enemy waved their bayonets and charged straight at us looking for a chest to pierce, a heart to break. We answered the same way. Dawn rose and the endless stretch of dead began to smell. We marched a long time and the air was cold. Soon it will be winter.

December 25, 1862
Camp Horsefood

Dear Diary,

Today we ate the last of our stock. We are now living on horses. It was hard to kill them because they worked on the farm, our only companions. The meat was hard and made many of us sick. We had to stack the dead bodies to keep us warm. It will be a hard winter if we keep out of battle because the North has the food stock. I fear another battle.

II
August 14, 1863
Battle of St. Mary

Dear Diary,

Today will be the last day of our regiment. The portal to hell has opened. The Yankees have come full force just to kill us, to hunt us like rats till there are none of us. Hundreds of them just to kill us. I waved my bayonet and fear came to us. I was plucked like a goose feather. I madly killed anything in my path. I do not know what I was doing but it found me. It took my left side and I fell to the ground. I lasted a day lying in pain, my body too weak to kill myself. Soon I too will be killed.

THE END

Koya Oneda, Grade 5
William Winchester Elementary, Westminster, Maryland

Not There Yet

In the 1800s women were treated like pretty dolls by men. They were nothing, zip, zero, they simply didn't matter. They wore corsets that pulled their stomach in and up to make them look pretty. These corsets also caused death, but the men didn't care, as long as their wives looked pretty. However in 1892 girls began to lose their doll image and were allowed to play basketball (Winning Ways 1996). Women have come a long way since then but aren't *there* yet. In 1989 an AFF study of television showed that 92% of televised sports are men, 3% are women and 5% are neutral topics (Winning Ways). Don't you think that women deserve more respect than that? Jackie Mitchell who struck out Babe Ruth or Toni Stone a baseball lover is unknown to the "normal" sports lover. Never heard of them? Well you just proved my point.

Corsets, dolls, cooking, not exactly paradise. But Paradise or not women's life was simply that. Everything was too hard for women and too easy for men. Women were so "fragile" that even riding a bike was a big deal (Winning Ways 1996). However they weren't even allowed to ride a bike until 1892 when Francis Willard decided that she wanted to know how to ride a bike. Also when women were riding a horse they had to sit sideways so they wouldn't go too fast and so their skirt wouldn't fly up (Winning Ways). As you can see women were truly treated like pretty dolls to men.

Women truly have come a long way since 1892 basketball. They started out playing basketball in a classroom with skirts. Eventually, girls were actually playing on basketball courts. During the first 20 years girls would play on outside grass courts during the summertime. Around 1912 the rule of women's basketball varied, making it hard on the girls to remember the rules. The rules varied because of the great concern with women playing basketball. People thought that women were more "selfish" and not as team oriented in team games as men (Women's Basketball Museum). As one of the rules women were forced to wear uniforms. These uniforms were a scarf, a skirt, and a blouse, which were uncomfortable to play basketball in (Women's Basketball Museum). But if you've seen women basketball players now, you know that the uniforms have changed. Around 1934 women started wearing shorts and tank-tops the color of their team with their team sign on the top of the front of the shirt, and believe me, they loved it compared to what they did have. As women's basketball progresses, countries all over the world (such as the Philippines) had women basketball games. Though you may not notice it, but if you really think about it, women's basketball is a game that deserves respect.

Women have always been progressing in everything they do. From 1892 basketball to the clothes they wear. Even today, they are trying to earn respect in sports. All women desire the same respect men receive but to me it's not happening. One thing that always has been a problem is how much women's sports are featured in the media. Not even *Sports Illustrated* shows women. In 1993, in 52 weeks of *Sports Illustrated* articles, only 6 women are pictured. The worst part was that one woman was a swimsuit model, two were wives of baseball players who were killed in boating accidents, and the other three were athletes who were the victims of violence (Winning Ways). Also the top ten readers' choice of 2001 had no women, not even the editor's choice had a woman until number 9 out of 10 (ESPN). Personally I think that that was because women aren't as televised as men. Even the women's college basketball finals were on channel 37.

Now honestly, who watches that channel? Also there were no advertisements for the women's basketball finals when there were at least 3 *different* commercials for the men's finals, which were by the way on channel 13. What would you watch, channel 13 or fuzzy channel 37? Rachel Krone from Mrs. Carhart's class quotes: Women are just as good as men but aren't as televised." "They don't get as much recognition from the media," says Mrs. Carhart (a fifth grade teacher at William Winchester Elementary School). "Women have truly progressed since the 1800s; they just haven't reached their goal yet."

Women everywhere are still fighting all the time. Whether it's fighting for respect or fighting against bad comments, women never give up. Women like Martina Navratilova who played women's tennis even when a sports writer claimed that if women learn to smash and volley a tennis ball the way men do they might destroy the image of tennis as a refined game, she kept on playing. Even Babe Didrickson was always fighting for respect and she was one of the greatest athletes of all time. However, in all of this fighting there is one thing that really bugs me. That's the fact that it's still going on today and it's still women struggling to earn their rights in the sports world.

Brittany Tyler
Grade 5
William Winchester Elementary
Westminster, Maryland